10
Lessons
of Life

Marc C. Bingham

10
Lessons
of Life

Marc C. Bingham

BLUE DIAMOND PUBLISHING

I want to thank my wife Debbie for her continued support and for encouraging me to write this book. My thanks also go to my family for putting up with me during those early years when I was so busy learning the basics of business, and to the Jaycees for helping teach me those skills. My heartfelt thanks go to my employees that believed in my leadership and dedicated their time and efforts to be the best of class in our field of business.

And finally, I want to thank my parents who taught me the value of hard work. My father always told me that if I worked harder than the other guy, I would never go hungry!

© 2019 Marc C. Bingham
Blue Diamond Publishing
All rights reserved. No part of this book may be reproduced in any form or by any means without written permission.
All photographs appear courtesy of the author.

Written by Rob Behunin
Compiled by Gregory Sheehan
Edited by Stephen G. Handy
Designed by John Gibby

Library of Congress Control Number: 2019917912
ISBN: 978-0-578-60375-9
Printed in the United States of America
Walsworth Press, Marceline, Missouri

CONTENTS

CONTENTS

INTRODUCTION

Some people are born lucky.

Well, actually, I don't know for sure.

Maybe I am one of the lucky ones.

Maybe you're one of the lucky ones.

To be perfectly honest, in some sense, we are all the lucky ones.

I WOULDN'T HAVE GUESSED I WAS LUCKY when I was four years old and nearly died from a childhood mishap. I wouldn't have guessed I was lucky when bankruptcy was just a phone call away. I wouldn't have guessed I was lucky when divorce nearly unhinged my world, the way it has, or may, with many of you.

When I drive by a local park and see homeless people wandering around I realize they are at ground zero in life and I contrast that scene with my life. There were times when I was at ground zero in dollars and burdened with $10 million in debt from business mistakes I'd made. It's a stark contrast to think that a homeless guy might be worth $10 million more than you because he has zero debt and you have so much debt you don't know how to get back to break even.

Or maybe one day you realize you're actually doing great and have money in the bank but you haven't gone through your first divorce yet. You will soon find out how quickly your empire can dissolve.

Maybe I was lucky after leaving Idaho Fish and Game when my replacement and another biologist, were killed by Claude Dallas. Maybe

I was lucky that I left the U.S. Fish and Wildlife Service in Wyoming for the Bureau of Land Management and shortly after the one that took over my position and two others were killed in a freak, mid-air collision while flying my usual depredation run. Maybe I was lucky I wasn't on my helicopter with a friend when it suddenly plummeted to earth.

Luck. Fate. I'm not sure.

After all is said and done, as I look back on my life, I believe we create our own luck. The harder and smarter we work, the luckier we'll be. My dad once told me, "It's not what you have or possess. It's who you are. Do your absolute best in life and give it your all." My parents taught me the value of hard work, and I am eternally grateful to them for that lesson and for all the "luck" that has come along putting that lesson into action.

Over the years, I've learned a few things about work, about jobs, about careers—mostly by trial and error, heavy emphasis on the error. I have clawed my way out of pitfalls, crags, and ravines, and each time I have learned a different way to look at life and business. As a result, I have developed a set of principles that have helped me work harder and smarter—principles that have helped me capture that illusive creature, luck.

Was it luck that our company was named by Inc. Magazine in 1981, 1982 and 1983 as one of the fastest growing companies in America? Attending their annual conventions since then have been great and I've learned a great deal about how to be "lucky."

At this point in my life, I want to pass my experience and my message on to future generations. I share what I've learned to honor my parents. I do this also because my wife, Debbie, encouraged me to do it. I do this for my friends, with whom I have shared many of the things in this book. Some of them consider themselves the lucky ones.

I've never intended to keep things a secret. On the contrary, I've been looking for a way to share my story and the things I have learned with others.

I hope you enjoy this book.

L'chaim.

Marc C. Bingham

When the Pages Were Yellow

CHAPTER 1

THE SMELL OF ETHER

I WAS BORN IN 1940, just before the United States entered World War II, on Indian Bench near Roosevelt, Utah.

Most of you reading this book won't even know where that is. Lots of people in Utah won't know where that is either.

I've been told that the first explorers who came out and surveyed the area we call the Uintah Basin reported back to their bosses that "the only purpose for the land in that area is to be another piece of the earth's crust."

Sounds a bit bleak, doesn't it?

It's really not—not bleak at all.

Try this: Leave Salt Lake City and head east on I-80. Go past Park City, get on Highway 40 and pass Heber City. Wander through Daniel's Canyon (what an amazing, beautiful canyon, watch for moose!) and slide by Strawberry Reservoir (flat and crisp as glass—be sure to watch for elk and deer in the open spaces), and just before you get to Duchesne, stop and admire Starvation Reservoir for a minute (it's like a little Lake Powell), and as you make your way from Roosevelt and on to Vernal, look north: the high Uinta Mountains are there—lakes, rivers, streams, fish, wildlife, open spaces, clean air. This was and is my home to this day.

When you get to Vernal, you can go see the pets I grew up with— the dinosaurs! (That's what my kids like to say.) But you should really go see the old Bank of Vernal, that is now Zions Bank. I think it represents the grit and the innovation of the people in the Uintah Basin. You see, when the Bank of Vernal was built, they wanted a brick exterior. The only bricks available were in Salt Lake City. Shipping the bricks by commercial freight wagons was way too expensive, but sending them parcel post was about half the cost. So, tens of thousands of bricks were individually wrapped and sent through the mail from Salt Lake City to Vernal.

Can you imagine thousands of bricks piled up in the post office? Word on the street was that the postmaster at the time was so fed up with all the bricks coming in that he sent a colorful telegram to Washington D.C. saying, "Some son-of-a-bitch is trying to mail an entire building through the U.S. Mail!"

Before the postmaster general could remedy the situation (government even moved slowly back then) the bricks were all shipped and in place.

I love that story and I'm sorry for the diversion, but I think demonstrates that sometimes you just have to do what it takes, crazy as it sounds, to get things done.

So, when I was born in the Uintah Basin, America was digging its way out of the Great Depression. In our town, poverty was everywhere. There were shortages of all kinds. We all made sacrifices. We went without. It was a tough time for Americans, but we were a tough people. The biggest event of my early childhood was the Second World War, and in many ways gearing up for the war helped America out of its slump and into an era of prosperity. I remember the day when running water and electricity were installed in my home. Up until that time, we had no central heat, no running water, and cooked on a wood stove.

Towards the end of 1944, I came face-to-face with death. My family lived in Alteria, Utah, half-way between Vernal and Roosevelt. My mother was out gathering cows, and my dad was working away from home. I was a precocious and enterprising child. Ok. I was a rascal—plain and simple. You know the type. On this occasion, while my mother was out gathering cows, I scaled the kitchen counter like a squirrel and retrieved the matches my mother had hidden in the high cupboards.

With the matches clenched in my chubby little hand, I immediately went to the front yard and built a small fire. It didn't stay small for long, so I tried stamping it out. The fire caught the frayed and ragged edge of my pant leg. Stop, drop, and roll had not been invented yet, and I ran to the irrigation canal a few yards away, fanning the flames as I went. My pant leg acted like a chimney and drew the flames up my leg and all the way to my buttocks, melting the flesh.

I was scared, but I do not remember feeling any pain, even as I jumped into irrigation canal. The fire, sure enough, had burned the flesh, but it had also seared the nerve endings.

I don't remember crying.

I got out of the ditch. I was cold and shivering so hard my bones rattled as I tried to walk stiff-legged. My pants pulled at the melted flesh.

Again, I don't remember crying. I was lucky.

I grabbed a blanket, wrapped myself up, and went and sat in an old shed. I knew I was hurt pretty bad, and all I could think of is how much worse things would be when my mother came home.

About an hour later, maybe longer, my mother came looking for me. She found me in the shed, still cocooned in the blanket. All I could think about was the trouble that awaited me. In a feeble attempt to avoid the inevitable—whatever that might be—I told my mother that I had a bad sunburn. She didn't believe me for a second. The smell and my charred pants confirmed her suspicions.

I was transported to an old country doctor who peeled off my pants and started bandaging me up just to keep the burns clean. Again, I don't remember crying. He told my parents to bring me back the next day. There wasn't extensive medical expertise in Roosevelt, and the prospects of my recovery were bleak at best.

Looking back, what saved me, ironically, was the war. A doctor who worked at the burn center in Ogden was on reassignment to the burn center in Denver, and his travels took him right through Roosevelt and Vernal via Highway 40. He happened to be at a filling station and heard about a little boy who was badly burned and asked if he could see me.

How lucky was I?

He took one look at me and told my parents that if they did not get me to the Ogden burn center they would lose me.

It took three and a half hours to get to Ogden. My condition, serious at that point, required that I stay in the burn center for nearly four months. Surgeries, skin grafts, more surgeries and more skin grafts. My room smelled like a burnt roast. From time to time, they nurses moved me to a different room. My parents said they could always find me by following the smell. It was questionable whether or not I could keep my leg; but because the skin across my kneecap had not been damaged, I avoided amputation.

It took years for my leg to heal. Grafts had to be routinely redone. Even after my leg healed, it was easily reinjured when I played sports. Seems like I had a perpetual scab on my shin for years and years. While the scabs and scars are long gone, the memory still lingers. Whenever I smell a diesel engine, I remember my first experience with fire. We used ether to start a diesel engine on a cold Uintah Basin morning, the same type of ether they used in the burn center to put me to sleep so they could cut, scrape, clean, and repair my leg.

All in all, it was a long and painful lesson, a lesson that forever shaped my life.

The incident with matches, my leg, and the burn center prompted my parents to rethink living in Alteria. They thought it might be better to raise me in a bigger community, a city with fewer matches. My father had a friend who was doing construction work in Oakland, California, so we moved. It was nice for a couple of years, but, truthfully, we all

THE SMELL OF ETHER

got homesick for the Basin, and we didn't waste any time hustling back. We made it back just in time for me to start the second grade. It felt good to be back in a rural setting, back to nature, open spaces, plenty of places to run free.

Many of the outlying communities had their own elementary schools. They were small, we all knew each other—probably too well—but is was a good to have such personalized attention and more freedom than we did in California.

We were bused to Vernal for junior high and high school, and on really cold mornings when the bus stopped to pick me up, I swear I could smell the ether used to start that old diesel engine.

By the time I was in sixth grade I, along with one other kid, was the king-bee of the central school (if there is such a thing as a "king-bee"). Everybody knew we were the head of the pack—the alpha dogs. Then, when we hit seventh grade, students from six other schools were added to the junior high mix and then combined with the high school. The pecking order was ruined and fighting for top spot began as the king-bees from seven different schools tried to sort out a new hierarchy. It took nearly that whole first year—all of seventh grade—before we had it all sorted out. It was my first real experience with politics, and for the first three or four of those months, I handled it pretty well. I came home every night with a torn shirt, which made my mother furious!

When I started the ninth grade, Vernal had built a new high school and the ninth graders were kept with the seventh and eighth graders instead of going on to the high school. By this point, there were five of us boys who were considered the leaders of the school, all of us jocks and into sports. That year I was very impressed by a kid there who was older than me, a "Big Senior" in my mind. His name was Terry Anderson, and he was my first hero. He was a great athlete, a track star and an all-star basketball player, and of course, football player. I watched him closely. He was a good-looking guy and always had a girlfriend. I would go over to the high school and stand in front of the trophy case, just staring at Terry's name, which was on 18 different trophies in the case. He was my idol.

7

Even though my leg pained and nagged me throughout my childhood and into my adolescent years, I loved to run. I could easily out run all my classmates and I had good hands. I was active in athletic programs and when I landed in high school, I decided to follow in Terry's footsteps and play football. It was my dream to be a receiver, to catch the winning touchdown in the "big-game" and have my name on trophies in the trophy case too. The problem, however, was that we lacked a competent, skilled quarterback. We didn't have a quarterback who could throw that game-winning pass. The quarterback we had just didn't have the right "head" for the game. He didn't think well on his feet or in pressure situations.

I used to moan and complain to my friends and my family, "Gee, if we'd just called this pass play we coulda won the game." My constant complaining didn't get me anywhere (except to the 50 yard line of total frustration!) or the team either. So, I gave up my desire to be a receiver and tried out for quarterback because I thought I was the better "thinker."

I worked hard, studied the playbook, threw passes to friends and, of course, rallied the support of my friends. I succeeded, and I held the quarterback position all through high school, and, boy, I could run if given the chance.

During my junior year, we only lost two games, but we didn't make it to the finals. In my senior year, however, we took the region and went on to play in the state championship against the team from Cedar City, Utah. The game was held in the late fall, just after a blizzard had dumped 14 inches of snow on the field. When the game started, it was still snowing, and the officials were concerned. There was talk of flipping a coin to see who would be the champions. I couldn't stand the thought of my dream of playing in a championship being decided by a coin toss. Lucky for me, the crowd was more upset about the idea of a coin flip than I was and kept chanting, "Let them play!" The game went on.

It was a slow, slippery game. Cedar City scored early and missed their extra point. Then we scored and it was 6 to 7. Cedar scored again and again missed their extra point: 12 to 7. For the rest of the game we traded play after play in a blinding snow storm, neither team putting points on the board.

It was brutal. Everybody was soaking wet and cold. Our wingback slipped and was out of the game. Both sides were out of time outs.

With 30 seconds left in the game, we were in scoring position. My tightend and I worked out a play to get him in the clear and in the end zone. He was sure he could get open and score. I called the play, the ball was snapped, and life went into slow motion. I watched the defensive pressure coming towards me: it was weak, scattered, and there were open running lanes. I looked left for my tight end and he was open near the end zone.

Pass or run? Both good options. I had a good, clear lane. I could make it. I knew it.

I stepped back and made the pass.

The ball hit the receiver right on the numbers but he broke the cardinal rule of receivers: Don't run until you catch the ball. My receiver dropped the ball and the hope of winning the championship game was lost.

I've relived that play over and over in my mind. I could have run the ball. I had an open lane. It taught me a great lesson. We all have decisions to make. We make those decisions and then we live with the consequences.

I've made my peace with that experience, and since then I have relived it many times over. In my personal life, family life and business life, I have stood under pressure, in the blinding snow storms and squalls of life, and had to decide, "Pass or run?" And what I have learned is that with either "pass or run" there will be consequences. We don't always make the right call. However, what matters is that we are brave enough to accept the challenge and responsibility to stand up under pressure, do the difficult thing and then deal with consequences, move forward, and make the best out of whatever happens.

I think President Teddy Roosevelt, a great outdoorsman and statesman, said it best:

"It is not the critic who counts; not the man who points out how the strong man stumbles, or where the doer of deeds could have done them better. The credit belongs to the man who is actually in the arena, whose face is marred by dust and sweat and blood; who strives valiantly; who errs, who comes short again and again, because there is no effort without error and shortcoming; but who does actually strive to do the deeds; who knows great enthusiasms, the great devotions; who spends himself in a worthy cause; who at the best knows in the end the triumph of high achievement, and who at the worst, if he fails, at least fails while daring greatly, so that his place shall never be with those cold and timid souls who neither know victory nor defeat."

CHAPTER 2

FINDING MY DIRECTION

Even though I had been a leader all through high school, though not always realizing it, I really was somewhat of a loner. I liked to get away and be by myself. I hiked all across the high Uinta Mountains of Utah during the summer months. I traveled to countless mountain lakes, looking for the biggest fish. Some Sunday afternoons I found myself 18 to 20 miles away from my truck at three in the afternoon. Sometimes I didn't get back to my truck until 10 or 11 at night because I had to cross over 10,000 feet to 12,000 feet mountains. What I learned, saw and experienced on those private excursions, day and night, stuck with me, teaching and conditioning me for the future.

In high school, I liked football and basketball well enough, but let's face it: I'm not overly tall and if I tried to weigh 250 lbs., I'd have to find a way to defy the laws of gravity. Track was my real passion and it was where I really excelled. It suited me better. It was something I could do alone. Me against the competition.

My sophomore year, Dean Lundell and I broke some of the state records at the Brigham Young University Track Invitational in Provo, Utah. Dean was the first high school student in Utah to run the 880-yard dash—the half-mile—in under two minutes. I ran the quarter mile—the 440—in 50.1 seconds—on a cinder track, by the way! Dean and I were part of the team that broke the medley-relay record by six seconds. It was the oldest record on the books at that time.

I loved track, but track wasn't going to pay as a career. Still, it did help me go to college because I received a track scholarship to Utah State University in Logan, Utah. I started my freshman year there in 1959.

What amazed me was that training for the track team began in the fall even though the track season wouldn't start until spring. I still remember running wind sprints that first season. Suddenly I was a small fish in a very big pond, which included African-American athletes. They were talented. The caliber of my competition had taken a huge leap forward. I found that my quarter-mile in college seemed somehow longer than in high school, about 40 yards too long, which taught me an important lesson about competition: there's always someone out there who is better than you, and records can always be broken.

Exhausted from all the training, I would go home and lay down for a few minutes, which turned into more than a few. Before long, my studies gave way to ample afternoon naps. On top of the effort of track, courses were harder than in high school. And then there was the complication of having too much fun. I was meeting people, living a social life that I had somewhat denied myself in high school. I began making connections, some of which have lasted for a long time.

My grades began slipping in the first quarter of my college career. At first I didn't realize that taking 21 credit hours and being on the track team and being a social person would take such a toll. Coming out of high school my GPA was about a 3.75. That first term in college it dropped to 1.67, a D+.

For the first time in my life I was a below average person.

Me—Mr. King-Bee, Mr. Quarterback, Mr. "I Never Took a Book Home from High School To Study Anything Ever!"

Now, "Mr. Below Average."

This was something I was not used to and something I didn't know how to handle.

But I finally snapped out of it as I drew inspiration from my family. I remembered that as the oldest child, I had younger brothers and sisters who expected me to be an example. I decided that although athletics were important I'd better hit the books and learn how to study.

However, in college the coursework was different. The teachers didn't care if I passed or failed. I dropped track and lost my scholarship in hopes of being able to spend more time studying, which I did. Unfortunately, I didn't do much better the next quarter. With a GPA of 1.72 I was put on academic probation. I was studying hard and working hard and dropped a few more classes. I got a lot of Cs, but one lingering D kept me at 1.99. I stayed on academic probation.

By my junior year, I was maintaining a 2.01 and still dating my high school sweetheart. We finally decided to get married, so I quit spring quarter to make some money. I went home to Vernal and took a job as a roustabout hand, which was unskilled labor, in the oil fields. Pretty quickly, I was in charge of the seven-man crew laying pipe for a high-pressure gas line.

I was excited. I was in charge. I knew how do get things done. Confident and bold, I went right out and hired a couple of buddies.

Big mistake!

They just wanted to have fun, but I needed the job and wanted to keep it. I told them we could have fun or we could work. They chose to have fun. I should have learned my lesson then but it was many years— and many bad hires later—before I really understood the concept of getting the right people in the right seats on the right bus and going in the right direction. I realized that I needed to let my buddies go and hired people who wanted to work.

For the new crew, I set the job up as a game: "Let's see how many breaks we can take in a day," I told them. After all, everyone likes break time, right? We'd go through each member of the crew, laying 10 joints of pipe, each changing positions for the next ten, until we had each completed one rotation. We would then take a 45-minute break. This built a great crew. We could lay about a mile and a half more pipe than any other crew. We laid a lot of pipe, took a lot of breaks, made money, made our bosses happy and I learned a lot about work and people and how to motivate them.

Eventually I knew it was time to get back to school, so my wife and I went back to Logan. Finishing my junior year, my grades started improving. My senior year I found myself short on credits. I needed 171 credits to graduate but I had only 141. So I took 21 hours in the classroom and nine hours of correspondence classes. I might have returned to my freshman-year grades under that load had I not had a supportive wife. She helped me study for the correspondence classes and in my last quarter I made a 3.0 and the Dean's List. My overall GPA went up to 2.5. Meanwhile, my first son was born. I graduated with a B.S. degree in wildlife management and the only business classes I took were applied statistics, where I earned a C. I got a D in economics.

What had I graduated in? It certainly wasn't business. But I learned the value of education. I had gained experience and knowledge that I owned. It was mine and nobody could ever take that away. More importantly, it is one of my greatest assets, and I have used that knowledge to better myself, my life and those around me ever since.

By the end of college I was ready to go out and live the dream of working in the outdoors. All through school I'd known a conservation officer for the Utah Fish and Game Department. I saw him often because I was always fishing, especially on the weekends in the summer. During the school year, my friends would be at the dances but I would be off somewhere in the High Unitas. When I was finishing up my education, the thought occurred to me that I wanted to work as a conservation officer. I loved the outdoors so working in the wilderness would be perfect.

Toward the end of college, spring of 1963, I took a bunch of placement tests. One of those was for the Idaho Fish and Game Department; I placed third. Unfortunately, they only hired the first two candidates. Thankfully, I had also applied to the U.S. Fish and

Wildlife Service and was hired to work in Arizona. Tucson became my duty station but during the summer months I was stationed in the mountains around Heber, Arizona, right on top of the Mogollon Rim (Louis L 'Amour country). I was a government trapper, catching coyotes to protect the sheep of local ranchers. I covered the area from Winslow to Snowflake and over to Showlow and interacted a lot with ranchers.

One of the ranchers I knew was a real "gun-slinger," and a woman. She was her own force to be reckoned with and had inherited the ranch from her father. Right after his passing, she went out to one of the local bars and got stone-faced drunk and pregnant. Twins. Twin boys, to boot. Rumor has it that not long after the boys were born she branded them—docked 'em— just like she did the sheep. In my day and my time the West was still wild!

During the winter I spent in Tucson, I decided to check on job opportunities in Idaho. When I called they told me there was a position open so in 1964 I left the federal government and went to work for the state of Idaho.

I was stationed in Burley where I met a lot of interesting people. After about a year and half in Burley, I was reassigned to Cascade, Idaho. With all of the "poaching" I had done in my high school years, I had learned all the tricks. Now as a conservation officer I made a lot of arrests because I knew the other side. I turned out to be a pretty good officer. My time working for the wildlife services is a perfect example of how being alert and open to learning new things helped me. While I wouldn't necessarily recommend becoming a poacher to learn how to be a better conservation officer, learning everything I could gave me more experience in my field and prepared me to be more successful than other officers.

On horseback, I patrolled the back-country area from Big Creek down to the South Fork of the Salmon, up through Soldier Bar to Cold Meadows, through the Chamberlin Basin, and over to Mackay Bar and Bergdorf Summit. I was in the back country for six weeks at a time and I was in heaven!

I had an interesting experience in that back country when the Baltimore Orioles came into the area after they lost the 1964 or '65 pennant. I happened to come into their camp and noticed they had several elk hanging without tags. I had no choice but to arrest the whole team!

Through the experience we actually became pretty good friends. They knew the law and they'd been caught; they were pretty good-natured about it. Later, I was flown—by the Orioles in their own DC-3—to Idaho City for their trial. The judge fined them only $25 each. Then they flew me back into my wilderness area. I'm pretty sure the judge got autographs!

To this day, I don't know why they just didn't push me out of the plane! No one would have ever found the body. In fact, they were all laughing over the incident. I thought it was a big coup to arrest that many famous baseball players, but maybe they'd been through that kind of situation before – and what's $25 to a pro ball player even in 1965?

Winter in Cascade began the first of November, and heavy snows and high elevations made sure winter didn't end until the first of June. During my years there, we didn't really have snow machines except for an old Skidoo that had a 9.8 horsepower engine. It was one of the first snowmobiles on the market.

One year a man was reported missing near Rocky Bar and we went in to look for him. He was supposed to be in the area watching people's properties and keeping snow off the roofs of cabins. The first officers who searched flew over but didn't see any smoke coming from any of the cabins, so they sent us in on foot to look around. We didn't find him and stopped for lunch leaving some orange peels on the snow. When we went in the next spring we found him about 20 feet away from our little piles. He had been completely hidden under the snow. It was later determined he died of a heart attack.

I felt horrible. Why didn't I look harder? As we live life, we never know how it will end or when. I learned early on "Do it now! Don't wait!"

Cascade offered my wife and me the "opportunity" to be homebound during the winter months. The only way we could really get to town for groceries was to walk to the main road and then hitchhike from there. The only other alternative was to walk through the waist-deep snow the entire way. Still, something good happened in that little town of less than a 1,000 people. I got to spend time with my small family of two boys. Then we added a third.

All the same, the pregnancy in Cascade was not a pleasant experience. We decided we did not want to spend another winter there. Since the state of Idaho was not responsive to my request for a transfer, I reapplied to the U.S. Fish and Wildlife Service and got a job. They sent us to Casper, Wyoming where I shot coyotes out of the back of a super cub airplane for the next year.

I also set a lot of traps, which I'm good at.

In the spring, I did a lot of what is called "denning." I'd follow the tracks of the coyotes to their dens. When I found them, I'd dig the pups out and destroy them. That part of Wyoming is a huge sheep area and all the federal forest service officers were tasked with protecting the local economy, which didn't include coyotes. Local ranchers paid enough fees to allow their sheep to graze on federal lands, so the government was duty-bound to protect the sheep.

After I'd been there about a year, the Bureau of Land Management started their Multiple Use Program and I applied. The Multiple Use Program included the management of the land for timber, mineral, watershed, range land, recreation, wildlife protection and fire control. I was accepted to the program and sent to Price, Utah as a wildlife and fire control agent.

This change, little did I realize at the time, would reshape my life forever.

During the two months it would take to process my transfer to Price, I became an oiler for Shimkat, a heavy equipment operator working on the interstate highway system. Granted, I could have just lounged around for a few months, but that's not my way. I have to be busy—ask anyone who really knows me. Oh, sure, I play hard at the right time, but I am at my best when I am busy and productive. Besides, I was raising a family. We needed the money and there was no reason for me to bum money off family and friends so I went to work.

Oiling is not glamorous. My job was to oil the machinery and I had to leave my wife and kids for two months to do it. The company was building a portion of the new I-25 highway from Casper over to Shoshone. Our home base was in Kaycee, Wyoming, which was easily the smallest town I had been in—no more than 200 total residents. Just after I got there, one of the supervisors said, "Why don't you just stay with me, and we'll share a room?"

This particular job started to teach me the importance of a saying my parents had often shared: "You can send more out the back door in a teaspoon than you can get in the front door with a scoop shovel." The idea is that, if you're sloppy or wasteful, you'll end up tossing out far more in money and resources than you can ever bring in. Think about it from the standpoint that a $1 soda at lunch every day adds up to $365 per year; that's a decent chunk of Christmas money for many people and it's just being thrown out the back door. I learned to be resourceful at this job, taking advantage of opportunities that came up and making sure I wasn't throwing money out the back door.

One experience on the job, dealing with deer, of course, really helped cement this thrifty way of thinking.

My day started at four in the afternoon. I'd work a few hours until "lunch" at 8 or 9 p.m. and then get off about 1 or 2 a.m. We were putting in a big multi-plate under the highway. A multi-plate is a galvanized, corrugated-iron product that is fabricated in curved segments so that individual pieces can be bolted together in the field to form a load-bearing arch.

While I was putting in this pipe, I noticed a number of deer. I had a spotlight on my vehicle so I could do vehicle maintenance at night and frequently caught deer in the light. My supervisor and I decided we should shoot the deer and eat them. I had plenty of hunting experience so we would shoot the deer and hang them from the big multi-plate arch under the freeway. Before leaving for work, I would put a roast in the oven and soon found that I had a lot of meat left over so I made sandwiches. Then other workers began to request sandwiches so as a crew we were eating about a deer a week, which worked out to about 15 lunches every day.

That kind of thing would probably be considered criminal by today's standards, but back then we fed ourselves on those deer and saved a lot of money. I was learning that a little ingenuity can go a long way toward cutting bills. And again, we were avoiding the "back-door" costs associated with eating out every day or even buying lots of groceries.

Two months later and as 1967 rolled in, I was finally working in Price and was assigned to set the browse transects, which means I was to determine the number of deer that needed to be carried over from one season to the next by marking the plant growth to see what percentage of it had been eaten. We would measure in the fall and then again in the spring. If the plants were being overeaten it was time to thin the herd. That kept me busy in the spring and fall working with all federal, state and local agencies.

During the summer season I was mainly concerned with fire control. That was a big job in the dry climate of Utah and we'd recruit a lot of people to work the fire lines. When we were overstaffed on the fire crews, we sent the extras to Alaska. Fires in Alaska didn't do any damage that anyone was worried about but the smoke and haze wreaked havoc with the military's radar systems. At that time, the Cold War was still on and the U.S. Government wanted to be able to see what was going on in Russia. The military was worried about a surprise attack coming eastward across the Bering Strait so they needed to keep the air clear.

I was one of the fortunate few because I got to go to Alaska. Alaska had plenty of local people to fight the actual fires. What they really needed were people to run the operations and train the locals. At one point I was assigned to a fire so a group of us flew up from Salt Lake City, went out on the fire-line for 36 days with no relief, marched back to Fairbanks, and, without even a chance to shower, flew back to Salt Lake City. You couldn't tell anyone's race by the time we got back; we were all the color of smoke. The odor must've been something. I never felt so dirty in my life and I've never felt that dirty since. Still, after seeing Alaska I knew I would return. It was such a beautiful area—with so much opportunity.

After some time back in Price, I met up with a guy I'd known in high school. If you'd taken the top five most popular people in the school (of which I was one) as the top of a pyramid, this guy would have been somewhere in the middle. He hadn't been the most social or the most popular guy back then. Thankfully, however, I still knew who he was. He invited me to a Jaycees meeting. Officially, the Jaycees are the United States Junior Chamber of Commerce (Junior Chamber = JC = Jaycee), but I told him that I'd seen the Jaycees during my time in Burley and all they did was party and I wasn't much of a party guy. He said they did much more than party and that I needed to come to one of the meetings. I declined, but he persisted. After he approached me about it three or four times, I gave in just to get him off my back. I wasn't going to join; I knew what my answer was going to be, or at least I thought I knew.

CHAPTER 3

SPEAK UP, JAYCEE!

A T THAT FIRST JAYCEE MEETING they were going through a program called "Speak-up Jaycee." The Speak-up program handbook described it as "a tool that can be used by your chapter to provide its members the opportunity to increase their abilities and confidence through practical experience." It teaches participants to learn and practice basic speaking skills, so that they can minimize the 'stage fright' experience.

In the first meeting I learned the Jaycee's model was "Leadership Training through Community Development." It was a program for young people age 21 and over and at the time consisted only of men. You were kicked out at age 35 having obtained the honor of "Exhausted Rooster." I quickly saw that what they were doing was a tremendous amount of good for the community and its members so I became very active.

My persistent friend was already a local officer there. I found that as far as networking and social structure was concerned, our roles from high school had reversed—he had passed me up as a strong leader in the local community and I was the one in middle of the pack. He was working for the U.S. Forest Service at that time and conducting the meetings at the Jaycees. I felt a little out-classed, but I wasn't about to stay down for long.

That's another lesson I've learned. Everybody makes mistakes, misses opportunities, or otherwise falls short once in a while, including successful people, rich people, the poor and the failures. The difference between those who make it and those who don't is that successful people refuse to stay down. They take their licks and get right back up, ready to try again. They'll keep going and keep trying new things until something sticks. I was starting to learn that, too, and during my first year as a Jaycee I watched and learned.

During my second year the federal government was moving a lot of their employees out of the area. The policy, at the time, was to move people every two years to make sure no one got into any bad habits, which was a bit disruptive, but effective. Perhaps I should have considered that in my own company later.

The unfortunate side effect of those transfers was that it left the Jaycees in Price devoid of membership—only nine men were left in the group. I was elected president of the Price Jaycees and decided that my first priority would be focused on recruiting new members. By the end of my first year in office, our membership had more than quadrupled to 41 people. During that time, out of the 51 chapters in the state of Utah we became the number one chapter.

The reason I really connected with the Jaycees—and what is really unique about them— is the Jaycees Creed. It honestly changed my outlook on life. The creed states:

> "We believe that faith in God gives meaning and purpose to
>   human life;
> That the brotherhood of man transcends the sovereignty of
>   nations;
> That economic justice can best be won by free men through free
>   enterprise;
> That the government should be of laws rather than of men;
> That earth's great treasures lie in human personality;
> And service to humanity is the best work of life."

When I first heard the creed, it really hit me – we, as a nation, can't be all wrong if what the creed states is what life is supposed to be about. In addition, the creed also aligned with my personal beliefs. I had always believed the creed and this just put words to my beliefs. That's probably why it hit me so hard – my beliefs had actually been right all along.

A little while after joining the Jaycees I was able to meet the fellow who wrote the Jaycees Creed when he came through Price. His name is Henry Brownfield. It was toward the end of his life before he died early from a crippling disease. He told me that he had written almost the entire creed in one night and that it had just come to him. But it wasn't quite right at first; it wasn't complete. It took him about six months after that to finalize it. One of the important changes he made was adding the first line. After all, faith in God was the reason so many people came to this land and created this country in the first place— they wanted religious freedom. When you think about it that way, celebrating and recognizing that freedom seems like a natural part of any organization that springs up within this country. Most, if not all, of the early settlers, believed in the Bible and even the few who didn't still had a belief in God. The Bible is a pretty good crossroads and contains the basics for a life plan. The Jaycees believed strongly in having a life plan and pursuing it. As I said, learning and trying to live the Jaycees' Creed became a life-changing experience for me.

In the Jaycees, we learned to model legislation in the same way that our government does in passing laws. We did this at the Utah State Capitol in the House and Senate Chambers. Being part of the organization gave me a good foundation for seeing how our civic society is really set up. Understanding how society really worked became a huge benefit to me later when I needed to alter the "society" of my business in order to help it thrive.

As part of that civic training, I was able to meet then-governor Calvin Rampton, a Democrat. Since Price is located in Carbon County, and Carbon was one of only two counties in Utah at that time that was Democratic in their political leanings, I decided to get Governor

Rampton on the phone. He was sort of a hometown boy, and I figured he might be willing to come to Price to speak. He graciously consented to address our local chapter and did it on more than one occasion.

One of the other things that the Jaycees gave me was a method of writing down my life's goals. I had never really written them down before. I basically knew what I wanted to do and who I wanted to be, but I found that it was all a little vague until I started writing them down. As I thought about it and set my sights on orienting to the goals of the Jaycees, I found that there are five basic areas for goal-setting:

1. Mental
2. Physical
3. Spiritual
4. Social
5. Financial

Being balanced in all of these areas is like creating a salad with lots of variety – the more varied the ingredients you have, the better tasting and more nutritious it will be. Life is just like a well-balanced salad. I look around at most people and see that the balance is off for many, even if it's just a little. Many people are too concentrated in one area—say lots of lettuce—but they are missing or short on one of the other key areas of life—they forget the veggies, the dressing, or cheeses. They are not balanced, so their "salad" doesn't taste good. For most of these people, you can see it in the way they act. They may be too concerned about finances and not spending enough time on their spiritual welfare, for instance, and spend time instead searching for ways to fill that void in their life.

Another way to look at this need for balance is what I call the "Teeter-totter Effect." Take any person—with all his strengths and weaknesses—and put him in one seat. Then put another person in the other seat—one individual will naturally have one set of strengths and abilities different from the other person. Then, if you stand back and watch what happens over time, you will realize that they will usually balance each other out. The strengths of the one make up for the deficiencies of the other, and, where they might be both weak, their combined ability is enough to get by even when they can't excel. This concept is often labeled by the buzzword "synergy," and it's something I experienced early on through my association with the Jaycees and something I applied throughout my business career.

Starting out in a business, you kinda have to wear the various hats of the organization. Everything rests on you, and any business failure comes as a direct result of your personal failure. As the business begins to grow and you have to bring more people on board, you'll probably start by trying to find more people like yourself. This works (although it's not ideal) for the first little while. Eventually, you will need people that balance that other side of the teeter-totter; you need people who aren't like you to shore up your weak points, to lift you up so to speak.

We learn and grow through the efforts of others on our behalf in addition to our own efforts. I believe that we're supposed to help each other be successful. John Donne, was right when he wrote the immortal words: "No man is an island entire of himself."

We're not here to be salads of just lettuce or carrots or dressing. We're not here to ride the teeter-totter alone. Life is all about building relationships and helping each other out. In Donne's poem, he closes with the words, "Therefore, send not to know for whom the bell tolls; it tolls for thee." His message is that all our lives are intertwined. When someone passes out of this life, we're all lessened by that loss—in the same way that we are all enriched when a new life enters this world.

Being part of the Jaycees helped me to get my head on straight. While my life up until that point wasn't bad or off-track, I certainly wasn't living up to my potential. I was capable of so much more than being an effective conservation officer or helping the government monitor the wilderness areas around Price, Utah. The Jaycees helped me realize that I needed to chart a new course going forward.

Right after I left the Jaycees, I gave a speech to the local Chamber of Commerce in Price, sharing with them the values of what I'd learned from the organization. I stated that within five years I would be a millionaire because of what I'd learned from them. Here I was only making a $9,800 salary after 11 years with the Bureau of Land Management, and I was telling a group of established business owners that I was going to be a millionaire.

They just laughed. They had every right to do so.

However, I had just raised over $150,000 for the Jaycees and I figured that I could do at least that much for myself. Many years after that speech, I made a $500,000 donation to the local college there in Price. So who's laughing now? I know that the members of that chamber aren't laughing because many of the people who were there when I made that speech all those years ago came up to talk to me after I made the donation. They told me that they had never forgotten what I had said. None of them had believed that a random nobody working in Price could be a millionaire—especially not within five years. I think they were glad to be proven wrong, as many of those people had children going to that college.

CHAPTER 4

THE EXHAUSTED ROOSTER
GETS HIS SECOND WIND

As I reached the level of "Exhausted Rooster" in the Jaycees just prior to my 35th birthday, I had been receiving a lot of offers to join the Elks Club. I thought it might be an organization where I could take what I had learned in the Jaycees.

I was a bit off the mark.

It was all right, but it provided nowhere near the level of training and support that I had received from my immersion in the Jaycees. There I had learned, in addition to life-skills, methods of organization and leadership. I felt I possessed so much more motivation in the Jaycees. The Elks Club didn't cut it for me.

So, at age 35 I sat down and set goals for what the rest of my life would bring.

One of my early goals was that when I reached 65 years of age, I was going to retire and travel. This goal came partly from a time I had attended a convention in Hawaii. While there, I noticed that all of the people traveling were young—around my own age at the time. I didn't want to give up travel just because I got old. I discovered later in life that older people often give up and give in. Travel gets to be burdensome, so they just want to stay home. They don't keep up with their goals. I didn't want to be like them, so I reset my goal to travel in the many years before my retirement.

Around my 35th year, some significant things happened in my life that would change my whole vision of the future and taught me how things worked in the "real world." First, was my "graduation" from the Jaycees. I had learned so much during my time there, and I didn't want to waste all that new knowledge and skill.

Second, I heard about a fellow Bureau of Land Management employee who at 64 years of age was told by his supervisor that he was to be "promoted" and moved to Alaska—because they needed him up there. The man told the bureau he didn't want to go – his sons were graduating high school and starting college and families and he wanted to stay around to retire. The bureau countered with, "You're going to do what we tell you if you want your retirement."

That didn't sit well with me and I told myself right then and there that when I reached 64 I wasn't going to have some old S.O.B. telling me what to do. I knew from hearing this man's story that I needed to get out, to branch out on my own. I wanted flexibility and control over my life, not a boss to tell me what to do.

Finally, I couldn't see myself retiring on a government pension— at least, not a Bureau of Land Management pension. In any case, I had goals for retirement, and those goals required something more, something different. The recognition that I wanted to control my future demanded a career change. My catalyst for change came through a friend in the Jaycees who, at the time, worked for Mountain Bell.

While in the Jaycees I had helped promote a local pageant, Miss Carbon County, by selling ads in its program. This was one of the ways I had raised the $150,000 that got me boasting to the Chamber of Commerce about my entrepreneurial abilities. My friend who worked for Mountain Bell looked through the program and told me I could make a lot of money selling ads for the Yellow Pages. He then proceeded to tell me all about telephone books and how to sell advertising in them. Phonebooks are largely a thing of the past now, but at one point selling advertising in them was a very lucrative business. In fact, it gave AT&T an 86% profit and a complete monopoly.

I saw the potential for profit in what my friend was saying. I saw the bigger picture. So I quit my job with the government and decided to start my own business. Scary, right? Sure, it was terrifying. While I didn't want to be that guy who gets told he has to relocate at 64 years of age by the government bosses, I also didn't want to be that guy who chased an insane get rich quick scheme and ended up losing everything he had worked for thus far.

No one in my family had ever owned a business. They all just worked for other people and brought home whatever wage they could earn. I wasn't content with that. Part of me thought I must have been dropped off by a stork into the wrong family. I wanted to be out on my own and in charge of me. When I told my family that I quit the BLM after 11 years – that I had things to do with my life – they begged me to wait nine more years. If I just waited a little longer, I'd have my pension and everything. Then I could try something new with a safety net in place. But I wasn't prepared to wait—I didn't want to wait—because I knew I wouldn't have the ability, time, or energy to do what I needed to do if I waited.

That said, here's how it stacked up:

When I first graduated in 1963 from Utah State with my wildlife degree, the government paid me $4,400 per year, which would be about $36,000 in today's dollars. Even back then, it was pretty bleak. Of course, I also got a $12 per diem for when I was out in the field. That was the butter on the bread. My parents had taught me to watch my expenses and keep a tight fist around my money, so I was capable of living on $3 or $4 a day. The $8 or $9 dollar difference helped a lot—a couple thousand dollars extra per year if I was out enough. Of course, the downside was that I had to be out in the field away from home and family.

By contrast, a man starting out in engineering in 1963 received a starting salary of more like $9,500—more than double my salary (and significantly higher than mine even including my per diem). I kept thinking, what did they have that I didn't have? A few more calculus and math classes, some design classes, maybe. It took me too many years to realize that what I was earning was really just a starvation wage—just enough to stay alive but not really enough to thrive. I realized that I had to make more money somehow if I wanted to support the children that were arriving.

This realization was the final straw that drove me out of government work and into the private sector. I became an entrepreneur out of necessity. I couldn't survive on what I was making, my future plans called for more resources than I could set aside, and I didn't see any other career I could slide into very easily.

One of the things I learned through taking the big risk is that when you see an opportunity, you need to act. If you sit and wait for the "opportune time" you will miss out! I didn't know it at that point, but waiting nine years to get my pension would have cost me some key years that laid a vital and lucrative groundwork for my success. Because I was willing to push through the discomfort and uncertainty surrounding a new venture, I was able to take advantage of an opportunity that has, in many ways, defined my life.

As it turns out, putting off something that needs to happen now is a good way to make sure it never happens. If it's not so important that it needs to be worked on right away, it can't be that important at all, right? The longer you put something off, the more important—and more demanding—the status quo will become. If I'd waited those nine years, I'd have ended up too comfortable—no matter how miserable and unfulfilled—to make a break and try something new.

I'm not a literature guy, but I have smart friends who are. One of those friends share with me what Shakespeare wrote this about taking a risk:

There is a tide in the affairs of men.

Which, taken at the flood, leads on to fortune;
Omitted, all the voyage of their life
Is bound in shallows and in miseries.
On such a full sea are we now afloat,
And we must take the current when it serves,
Or lose our ventures.

JULIUS CAESAR ACT 4, SCENE 3, 218–224

I didn't want to lose my venture, so I took the tide!

Successful people don't put off high-value activities. When they find an opportunity worth acting on, they act. It's that simple. They call whomever they need to call, organize whatever resources they need to organize, and get going. People who fail, interestingly enough, strategize and plan out all the different resources and people they think they need to involve but do this almost as a way to delay taking any action. If you want to be successful, then stop putting off your high-value activities.

Cut yourself free from the safety net. It's not really keeping you safe. It's just holding you back.

CHAPTER 5

PHONE DIRECTORIES COMPANY

Let me set the stage for you as I began this new venture: It was 1971, and I had about $3,500 to my name or about $22,000 in today's dollars and it was all stuck in my government retirement account.

I used all of that money as the start-up capital for my new business: Phone Directories Company.

I had never run a business.

I had never really sold anything.

What did I really know about selling phonebook advertising? What did I know about the various sizes, items and production requirements? Not a damn thing.

But I did learn something about the phonebook industry that made me think I could do well. Do you know how the Yellow Pages came into being? Before I continue, let me share that with you.

If you take a look at the history of the whole phone directory concept, it has actually been an independent business from the very start—and one fraught with trouble. The reason that business directories started being printed on yellow paper in the first place was because of a paper shortage at the printer in Cheyenne, Wyoming. The printer had used all of the white paper for the regular, residential listings, so for the business listing section he had to improvise and decided to print on yellow paper.

The first "phonebook" in the early days of the telephone was printed on one sheet of paper and contained names only—no phone numbers—of the subscribers to telephone service in New Haven, Connecticut. There were no phone numbers to print back then because every call was operator-assisted. You couldn't call someone by dialing a number. You just lifted the receiver and told the operator the name of the person or company with whom you wanted to speak and she connected you. In fact, the old rotary phones, which allowed a person to place a direct call, didn't really catch on until the 1930s.

In 1886, Rueben H. Donnelley, an independent publisher, created the first yellow pages phone directory that featured business names categorized by the types of products and services provided. Previous listings were simply alphabetical. In grouping businesses by type of service, he effectively invented a new industry. In 1909, St. Louis produced the first yellow pages directory to add coupons. The first yellow pages ad had actually appeared earlier, in 1898, but it wasn't a part of any phone company directory. The phone companies saw it and figured that there was a lot of money to be made by adding advertising to their directories.

In the early days the phone companies co-mingled the yellow pages—the ad pages and business directory—with their white pages. They got away with a lot in those early years, even mandating that if you didn't pay for your yellow pages ad, they could take your phone out and cut off your service. Once it became clear how profitable the directories could be, the utilities began buying up the independents. The monopolies grew and grew until even the more stubborn independents had to ally themselves with the phone companies. At some point, they had to respect which side of the bread their butter was on.

The value of an ad in the yellow pages back in the day made sense if you stop to think about where the phonebook once sat in the era of plug-in rotary phones: right next to the telephone. It was used all the time. Calling friends even required the phonebook sometimes, at least until speed dialing became more popular. But the money was there because one ad would be viewed by just about everyone in the community time and time again.

Ads in the newspaper could not be considered as effective because a newspaper is looked at once (and that doesn't mean the entire newspaper) then thrown away or used for something else. After its one day of viewing, the newspaper is gone, along with its ads, forcing advertisers to buy again and again.

Radio and TV advertising also have their problems, even though at times they can be necessary. A radio or TV ad is heard only by those listening or watching and must be repeated frequently (at a tremendous cost) if you want the audience to remember anything about it. Unless an ad is funny or poignant, an audience soon forgets it—assuming they even get the message you are trying to portray in the first place. Do people watch an ad for an appliance repairman and think "I should write down this number in case my washing machine breaks down some day?" No. Unless their washing machine breaks down they don't need that information.

But in the heyday of the yellow pages, this type of advertising was different in a couple of key ways. First, the directory was always right there, at the customer's fingertips. "Let your fingers do the walking" was one of the most brilliant ad slogans ever. People kept the book right by the phone for when they needed something. A key to effective advertising is to get someone to see your ad when they have an existing need. That is the shortcoming of newspaper, radio, and television. When the washing machine breaks down, who were they going to call? Most people would go to their phonebook and look for the best-looking ad.

Second, the phonebook was usually printed annually. That meant the advertiser paid monthly or once a year to appear in the book. Other methods of advertising often required a regular, and sometimes constant infusion of funds. Isn't it easier to pay once and get a guaranteed ad for a year?

These ads were so important that some businesses just couldn't miss their ad in the yellow pages. Specialty service providers in particular—car care, appliance repair, law firms, even restaurants— viewed their yellow pages ad as their bread and butter.

At one time, the power of the Yellow Pages produced the highest rate of returns of any advertising budget. There wasn't another medium that could come close. Funny how the new generation doesn't even know what a phone directory is. Not sure they would even know how to use a rotary phone. But for nearly 50 years, the Yellow Pages were more than yellow—they were gold.

So, having learned all this about the phonebook business, I determined there was a huge need and I could see ways to innovate and make it better. I knew there was something there, something big if I could do it right and do it quickly.

Even though I could see the opportunity, I still had to set up a new business "on the run." Most businesses operate on a profit figure of less than 10 percent revenues. In most cases even 4 to 5 percent is tops. So when you spend $100 and lose it, that's a huge loss. It can take as much as $2,500 in sales to make up for that $100 loss. You can't do that too often and stay in business.

Luckily (there's that word, again, "lucky") I had some help.

My friend from the Jaycees was taking the Salt Lake phone books and breaking them out into the individual communities. So, I started selling ads for his phone books. It wasn't long before he told me that I should join the Emery and Carbon County books into one. At that time, 80 percent of the dollars earned in Emery County were spent in Carbon or Utah Counties, anyway. I thought that Carbon County businesses would probably jump at the opportunity to advertise to Emery residents and save money.

He also said that the books for Richfield, Cedar City, and St. George were going to be the most lucrative. At that point, Mountain Bell had those books combined into one. The problem was that the people in Richfield didn't shop in Cedar City or St. George because those places were too far away—and the same concept worked in reverse. No one wants to be looking at a list of businesses two hours away. I took his advice and split those books; I did the first one in Richfield, UT.

This was a great innovation, but I had to get even more creative—disruptive, even.

The next idea was to publish the books on a market-line basis instead of a utility-line basis. Now, what in the world does that mean?

Up until that time, phonebooks were usually published directly by the phone utility company. Phone companies would just publish a list of their subscribers and pay for the printing by charging businesses for ads inside the phone book. Because nearly every adult was flipping through the phone book at least once a week, it was critical for businesses to have an ad there. However, sometimes the phone utilities would have different subscriber coverage than the local businesses needed for their marketing.

If I found that the phone company was meeting the marketing needs for an area, then there was no need for me to be there and waste my time. When the utilities were not meeting the marketing needs, however, there was a big opportunity for me by either combining or splitting books. Either way, I could make residents prefer my book over the phone company's option.

Another change I brought to the phonebook business was to combine the white pages with the yellow pages—which was literally unheard of in the larger markets. Utility companies at that time typically published the white pages (residential numbers) separately from the yellow pages (business numbers). That meant that every home needed to have two books.

That was horribly inefficient, but it was even worse than that!

When I was doing phonebooks in Ohio, I found that there was one county that had six or seven phone companies, which meant six or seven sets of phone books. In one of the communities, Main Street divided the services of one company from the services of another. People in that little town had to have two completely different white and yellow page phonebooks just to make local calls. I went in and replaced those four books with a single phonebook. The convenience of our book made it the directory of choice and we convinced businesses to buy ads in our books at a huge savings to them and a huge profit for us.

By splitting out the Richfield, Cedar City, and St. George books, I saved the advertisers in each town about 60 percent of the previous rates for a yellow pages ad, and it would appear only in its own, isolated community. The way we pitched the concept was "you're getting an airline ticket for the price of a bus ticket." Our concept for the phonebook was so popular we had businesses begging for ad space.

We had made some significant innovations, but we weren't done yet. How about this next little twist? In our books we added the name of the wife alongside the name of the husband using local church directories as a reference. It worked out pretty well. We were cutting into a space that had been almost like a secret.

When we started, phone directories were a monopoly for the phone companies and they were making 86 percent profit. That left us a lot of room to come in and undercut their prices while still making a substantial profit.

Believe it or not, back in the early days, the phonebook ad salesman drove a Cadillac into town and broke $100 bills at the local bar. He was a hardcore independent contractor. With the monopoly that utility companies had over the phonebooks, the salesmen had the power to bully the local businessmen into purchasing ads. Those salesmen were ruthless in pursuit of bigger, costlier ads. Often, after they had closed a sale with a customer who already had an ad, the salesman would return to the office and bump the size of the ad up in order to charge the businessman more, then coerce the business owner into paying for it.

Of course, when Mountain Bell found out, they released these men from their contracts and began to make the phonebook ad salesmen their in-house employees. They also cut back on commissions, so "Ma

Bell" could have more control over what the salesmen did and how they did it.

Eventually, those terminated salesmen began to compete with the phone company by publishing a separate phone book. After all, they had excellent, albeit shady, sales techniques. When we started to compete we had to take some precautions. We would make up a dummy name—something fictitious—so that we then could tell if these other salesmen were stealing our listings for their own directories. In an effort to protect themselves from these shady salesmen, the phone companies began putting the copyright (©) symbol on their books. It was supposed to help protect against theft, and they began to sue the salesmen and their companies for copyright infringement. Of course, the salesmen and their companies would just turn around and counter-sue the phone companies for violation of Anti-Trust laws. There always seemed to be a lot of litigation in the industry. Attorneys made a lot of money in those days.

Times were tricky, and we had to watch our backs.

CHAPTER 6

DUMPSTER DIVING

WITH SO MUCH INFORMATION AVAILABLE to us today, you can't really appreciate how hard it was to get the information we needed to put together an accurate phone directory. Sometimes, the only way to get names for our directory was to call up the operator. So we had a dozen people all over town calling up every hour, but they were only able to get three names at a time. Slow and painful, it took a long time to put a phonebook together that way, but at least we knew that if the operator gave us the name and address, it was legitimate.

Still, I thought that there had to be an easier, faster way. I wasn't content doing things the way everyone else did. I didn't want to have the same level of success that everyone else was having; I wanted more. As the saying goes, "If you always do what you've always done, you'll always get what you've always got." So, I decided to break the mold and try something new.

I consider myself very resourceful and I found out the physical location of the information operators. Their offices would get a new printout of names and numbers every month, which was for internal use only. When the month was over, the offices would get a new printout, and then they would take the old one and put it through a paper shredder and destroy it. I found out the date and time that the janitor would throw out the shredded printouts and then I'd go there and dig them out of the dumpster.

Using a light table, we could get the whole thing put back together in about 30 minutes or so (it was only about 50 to 100 pages for each city). Some people might think that we were stealing, but all we were doing was compiling publicly available information. After all, I could call the operator and get the same information—for free.

Our new way was just a bit faster, we used less of the operators' time, and we found some other great treasures in the dumpsters. To this day, I take my true friends dumpster diving.

Putting a phonebook together was hard—before the advent of the personal computer. It was tedious, and I won't bore you with all the details, but let me just give you a snapshot of what it was like.

To put a general phonebook together that included all the numbers for each town, we combined the numbers for each community into an alphabetized list with the aid of a typist who could type 130 words per minute. One person would sit on either side of her helping to alphabetize the entire directory as she typed.

What confused us at first was that for some of the listings on our reassembled-dumpster-lists there was a little box at the beginning of each name. Sometimes the box was blackened and sometimes it was empty. Also, some of the names or addressed were underlined. We found that, by calling the numbers to verify the listings, those that were underlined had either moved away or had their service terminated for non-payment. Those with the blackened boxes remained a mystery to us, but they were all working numbers, so we put them in the book.

However, we soon learned the secret behind the black boxes next to some of the listings: they were to indicate a non-published, private number. Phone company investigators immediately began looking for us to determine how we had put the phonebook together. We avoided them for months and still to this day they haven't figured out how we got the listings.

Our process was actually pretty simple. Our first printer was Southwest Offset in Dallas, Texas. The books were all laid out in what is called a "signature" format—four pages when printed and folded would become a book, face-to-face and back-to-back.

We used the Trailways bus system to get our printing master to them for their giant web-press. It took three days by bus to get it there. We would work all night getting the book camera-ready for printing in order to make sure it was on the 5:10 a.m. bus headed to Texas. Sometimes we got there just as the bus was ready to pull out—then those of us who had worked all night would go to breakfast. After breakfast we would go home to freshen up and maybe catch a two-hour nap. Then we'd start the process all over again on another directory for another area.

That's how a phonebook was born! I told you it wasn't pretty, and by today's standards it was clunky and inefficient. But for us, and by "us" I meant the 20 or so people that worked with me, our phone book innovations and platform worked. Not only did it work, it was very lucrative and something our advertisers and the public wanted.

We were doing well, but I knew it wouldn't always be that way. Things can change quickly.

CHAPTER 7

DAVIDS AND GOLIATHS

Technically my home address was in Price, at least that's where my family was. But my office was in Grand Junction. I took a small apartment above a bakery. I had one window on the world, and sometimes all I could see through the fog was the flashing yellow light in the intersection. I took a bath in the sink, slept in a sleeping bag, and was kept awake all hours of the morning by the mixers making the dough for the doughnuts. I imagined it is what being in a cement mixer is like. One morning the whole building shook so hard I chipped a tooth. I never got any free doughnuts, either.

I went home, to Price, most weekends.

I was working like crazy to get up to speed. Up to that point, I'd known wildlife, gestation periods, migration patterns, and how to thin a herd. But business? I didn't "know" a lick about how to run a business. Still, I had a sense of it, and I was willing to work hard to make the business thrive.

This willingness to work hard and keep trying, even if mistakes are made is another important lesson I learned: You must be willing to fight for what you want, otherwise someone else will want it more, and they'll take it before you can. Learn what you can, live with your decisions and don't be afraid to make mistakes. We all make mistakes from time to time. If you look at those errors in the right way, however, they can actually become your best teachers.

In a fairly recent movie, "Batman Begins," Bruce Wayne (Batman) falls down and breaks his leg as a child. His father (later quoted by the butler, Alfred) says, "Why do we fall, Bruce? So we can learn to pick ourselves up again." While the rest of the movie has little in common with real life, this quote rings very true. Life throws us all a curve ball every now and then. We all stumble and fall. We all make mistakes. The real difference between those who are successful and those who fail is that failures stay down when they fall down. Successful people get back up. It may not be pretty, but they'll do it. Successful people will get back up, clean themselves off, and get back to work. Learn to take your lumps and learn to roll with the punches, as I did when one of those company investigators out of Denver came after me.

In the process of putting a Colorado phone book together for the Grand Junction area, I discovered that a clear box next to a number meant that the number was to remain "unlisted," and the only way to get the number was by calling the operator at directory assistance. These numbers were not to be printed in the phonebook. In addition, as I noted previously, the mysterious black boxes that appeared next to some of the other numbers meant that neither directory assistance nor the phonebook could list or give out that non-published number.

When we mistakenly published those numbers, investigators for the phone company came looking for us. Their contracts with their telephone subscribers for privacy, verbal or otherwise, had been breached. We had listed about 3,000 numbers that were either supposed to be unpublished or unlisted and started getting calls from the people with those numbers demanding to know how we got them. We simply said that we got them from the phone company, which was true, though we'd taken the numbers without permission. Then those people called the phone company and complained.

Not long after that, I noticed a guy across the street from my Grand Junction apartment was watching me through a pair of binoculars. I never met him, fortunately, but I learned that his name was Ted Shields. He kept leaving business cards at my office asking for a meeting. I made some discreet inquiries about him and discovered that he was a phone company investigator, akin to someone from the FBI.

He watched me from daylight to dark—probably to figure out how I was putting the phone books together. When he would come over, I'd just slip out the back of the building. He never did confront me face to face. This went on for a week and I managed to elude him and finally went back to Price. During this time, I learned that the phone company (Mountain Bell) monopoly was determined to figure out how we got the phone numbers. It was clear that they felt they had a right to know what had happened.

I was learning to watch my step and be a bit more cautious. We had to find another work-around. Part of that work-around was using a double-keyed entry system, which entered each listing twice so that any errors in a listing could be visually caught.

In the mid-70s, when Contel, the Continental Telephone Company, a major competitor of AT&T and the Bell System, began putting fictitious names in each of their phone books, we were able to expose these fictitious names through the double-keyed entry system. Contel's strategy at that time, to keep guys like me from creating an independently published phone book, was to put 21 fake names in each of their books.

We deduced, however, that if we keyed in two different Contel books that we could figure out the fictitious names. It worked! Janet Breems, Arthur Andersen, Bruce Bradley were three of the names they included, who were simply Contel employees working in the Kansas office. When their numbers were dialed, the call would go to an intercept operator and all that was heard was a "click-click." It would never ring.

Once we had the list of fictitious names, we found that it never changed so we could tell which numbers and listings were false and didn't have to bother keying them in anymore. This saved thousands of dollars because we didn't have to verify each of Contel's directories.

With this double-keyed entry system, unless the error was in the original listing, our books became more accurate than the phone company's book. To help correct errors by the phone company, we put an ad in the paper stating that if a mistake in a resident or business listing appeared in a phonebook, people were to call a number, our number, and we would correct it.

Our methods were so thorough that we scared the big phone companies, and we actually got hit with copyright violations three or four different times. We would settle with the phone companies after we counter-sued them under the anti-trust laws, but it would still cost us about $300,000 per case. This was a tremendous burden on our little company.

One of our most powerful lawyers was Joseph Alioto, a big copyright attorney who wanted to run for president. He was so good, he could scare the phone companies into settling. Unfortunately, he didn't come cheap, charging us about $90,000 for his retainer, which was a lot of money in the 70s. That would be over a half a million today. We simply had to count it as a necessary cost of doing business. Between an original suit and our countersuit, it always cost us less to settle than hoping to win in court. Of course, the whole process was expensive for both parties, so settlements happened more frequently than not.

Eventually, I joined an organization called Associated American Directory Publishers (ADP). The small ADP group of independents got together in order to have the power to lobby against the major utility companies—Mountain Bell, Contel and AT&T. It wasn't much, but it began to level the playing field, mainly with the copyright issue, and the marketplace got a little less one-sided. For five to ten years we walked the halls of Congress to directly lobby for whatever equal rights or equal access to information we needed.

This was a huge distraction for us. The industry was awash in litigation, but we little guys stuck together. A large suit was brought between an independent company in Amarillo, Texas, called Great Western Directories Inc. and Southwestern-Bell. Southwestern maintained that they had done the work to get the listings and that if the independents wanted the listings they should have to pay $10 for each name, address, and phone number. Southwestern was trying to price the independents right out of the marketplace by basically calling what they printed in their phonebooks proprietary information.

I attended the trial in Texas. Great Western Directories had one attorney, a woman named Nancy Stone, who knew everything about the case—I would later hire her to represent me in a case in Alaska. Southwestern-Bell, on the other hand, had 20 attorneys—each who knew a little bit but did not have the whole picture.

It appeared to be pretty one-sided.

Great Western ended up winning that suit. Nancy blew Southwestern's attorneys—all 20 of them—out of the water and made them look like fools. It cost the phone company $21 million, and as a result, this litigation and another lawsuit in New York, the president of Southwestern lost his job.

They had the poor guy on record saying, "We'll, price those S.O.B.'s out of business."

We little guys had to keep fighting the big guys and dodging the bullets. It wasn't until 1991, and the lawsuit in Kansas between Feist Publications and Rural Telephone Service Company, that the question of copyright would be settled. This was a case that all the independent publishing companies got behind, and we took it all the way to the Supreme Court. The lower courts all sided with the telephone company and agreed that it could copyright its own phonebook. The Supreme Court, on the other hand, ruled that phonebooks, which held public information that was not particularly unique, could not be copyrighted. This ruling eventually caused some problems for the utility companies and their monopolies and became the first part of the Telephone Act that became law in 1996.

As easy as it was to retain the right lawyer to handle these copyright lawsuits, it was not easy handling the other challenges that we often faced. Just getting the information to print a book was sometimes extremely difficult, and dumpster diving finally went out fashion because of paper pulverizers rather than just shredders and enhanced security.

In Utah, for instance, our phonebooks were printed by linotype at Deseret Press in Salt Lake City. Linotype is a hard lead, old fashioned, grab-each-letter-and-place-it-in-a-block, kind of typesetting. It was slow, but effective when you needed to print in volume. Deseret Press printed copies of *The Book of Mormon* for the LDS Church part of the week and then printed our phone directories the rest of it. They did that for many years and the security at the Deseret Press was about as tough to get through as one of the national intelligence agencies.

The reason for all that security was that the phone directory industry was heating up. Between all the lawsuits there were a lot of companies trying to get a piece of the lucrative phone directory pie. That meant the people who had the information had power over the people who didn't. After all, it was ridiculous to think you could sell ads for your phonebook if you couldn't fill the phonebook with the names and numbers of the people in town.

So getting that information put me into a life of espionage—especially at the beginning and particularly in some of the smaller communities. The phonebooks in these smaller towns weren't available from any central entity, and the residents were a bit reticent to let you just roll into town and "borrow" one. The only way to get the phonebook was to drive hundreds of miles to the local library and check it out in person. And since the books were in the reference section they didn't check out very easily—unless there was a bathroom window handy. So, we had to come up with all kinds of creative ways to "obtain" the information we needed.

Sometimes the phonebooks could be "borrowed" from the utility companies themselves. You had to be a little bold, a little brave, a little gutsy, and just push your way through the receptionist. It worked by going to the company at lunch time, faking some sort of badge, and gaining access to their company library. If you were convincing enough, you could come out with several books at a time. The difficulty was that you couldn't go in as a visitor—visitors were escorted around, so you had to impersonate an employee.

At that point in time, I had nobody to do this for me, so it was up to me to acquire the necessary resources. It sounds a little shady, but you have to remember that we were trying to acquire public information, data that was available for anyone's use. I didn't look at it as stealing as much "procuring" this public information in order to grow my business. Furthermore, we didn't sell the phonebooks; they were given away free, so I wasn't profiting off the sale of this public information.

Why should I have to pay for a phonebook? No one else did. So I procured them through whatever methods I could think of. This worked for a while, but I quickly learned that I didn't know everything and that even my techniques could go stale.

CHAPTER 8

SALES AND SALESMANSHIP

IN THE EARLY DAYS—fresh out of my government job—I knew very little about sales, so I looked for models of the "great salesman." I quickly found that there was a very fine line between being a great salesman and being a crook or con-artist. I decided to stay on the salesman side. I wanted to return value for every dollar invested; I felt that I owed that much to my customers. It didn't take me very long to realize that the best way to grow my business was through repeat business, and the best way to get repeat business was through a satisfied customer who would then buy again. A disgruntled or angry customer could only be strung along for so long before going somewhere else.

What's more, an angry customer will tell far more people about a bad experience than a satisfied customer will talk about a good experience. It's a question of emotions. Angry customers are riding high on emotion, and that drives them to be vocal. Satisfied customers are content; they aren't driven to be vocal in the same way. If you want to be successful, you can't let your customers end up angry, and that means giving them value when they give you money.

In addition to giving value, a good salesman knows when to speak, when to shut up, and when to ask the closing question. I thought I was a pretty good salesman when I was making $200 in sales per week, including Saturdays. I was delivering value and staying true to my word. Customers seemed to like me. I thought things were going pretty well. Then I hired a woman who so far outdistanced me, it's almost embarrassing. She worked two, maybe three days a week and brought in $2,500 to $3,000. I was floored. Her results were more than 10 times my results in less than half the time. I asked her to come with me on some of my sales calls to give me some tips.

I took her to meet with an established client, one where I could show her how good I was. She kept kicking me under the table. By the end of our discussion, she had kicked me at least six times—maybe more! Then she took me outside and said, "You could have closed that guy, and all you did was blabber on and on. You talked your way in, and you talked your way back out."

Then she showed me a unique way to ask for the order. Once I learned her technique, I went from a $200-a-week salesman, to a $2,000-a-week salesman. She taught me to mock up the physical ad that I wanted to sell to a person so they could visualize it, then go in with a few well-placed pointed questions and the following "List of Sales Steps" firmly in mind. Now, there are lots of recipes for success when it comes to sales. Some are more sophisticated than others. Some are created and endorsed by Harvard business graduates. That's great. All I am saying is, this process worked for me selling phonebook ads.

The Approach. How you approach the customer is both a physical and a mental deal. It really is a "first impressions" situation. You've got to make it a positive experience for the potential client right from the start. Judgments and opinions are formed in the first few minutes of a meeting—even the first few seconds—and, once formed, they can be really hard to change. If you start off on the wrong foot, you've lost the sale even before you've asked for it. Also, before you ever go in, make sure you know as much as possible about the person. You want to meet with the person in charge who can write the check and close the deal. This may not be possible to do beforehand, but try anyway.

The Warm-up. This is the fact-finding phase of the sale. You need to find out who, what, when, where, why and how. Without this information, you can't craft the sale to the customer, which means you'll likely fail. If you come in with a smile but quickly switch to a frown, the customer will switch you off. So maintain an affable, interested attitude and try to find common ground with the customer. Make the conversation about them and their business, not about you. Make it easy for them to keep liking you.

The Qualifier. Make sure you're talking to the right person. If you take the first two steps and then discover you're talking to the wrong person, you've still got a chance that they're now on your side and will help you find the right person. Determine whether the contact is the decision-maker with authority over whatever you're selling and whether or not they can write the check. If they can, then you are talking to the right person. If they can't, you need to get the right individual on board. Time is money, so talking to the wrong person is just wasting both your time and money.

The Presentation. This step can be a tricky part of the process. Up until you are ready to present your product or service, you don't want to give the potential customer any real details. Your focus at the start is to win their trust—friendship even, if you can manage it. Then you shift gears and start telling them how your product will benefit them. Generally, this is best done by telling a little story about why you're affiliated with the company and what wonderful things you've seen with other customers. Stay general during this part. Then, as you can see them getting interested, tie in the parallels from what you've seen in the past to how your product can help them. It's not enough to tell them that another company saw a huge sales increase because they listed an ad in your phonebook; you have to help them visualize their own increase in sales by virtue of being in the best, most popular phonebook in town.

The Close. This is when you finally pull the trigger. At first, this can be a difficult step to time properly; it was certainly my problem when I was starting out. If you close too early, you'll get rejected; close too late and you'll have already ruined the deal. Your objective is to get them agreeing with you—nodding and such—because this tells you that they have the vision of what you're describing. Once you get that agreement then remind them of the program that you have presented.

Then comes the critical question. Don't ask them if they're interested; instead, you ask the question, "Is there anything that you want to change?" Then you shut up!

The first person who speaks after this point will be the loser. If nothing happens after about 30 seconds you start, silently, writing up the order. Silence is the same as permission to move forward. If you finish writing the order and nothing has been said by the customer, you can then ask, "Can I get your okay on that?" Fifty percent will come up with an objection at this point, so you handle the objection and then say, "Anything else you want to change?" Then you continue writing to give them a chance to think. Once they agree and start signing, you ask them if you can pick up a check now. Wait until they are halfway through their signature—past the point of no return—then sit back, leaving them all alone as they finish signing.

Once the pen leaves the paper, you stand up. But you still don't say a word. They will put the pen down, or they will write the check right then. Sometimes they will still have a final objection: "Do I have to pay for it all now?" Simply respond with, "How would you like to pay for it?" Typically with our ad sales, the salesman got paid a third of the commission up front, a third on the proof, and the final third upon publication. You know this, but let the customer suggest the terms. They will usually suggest something that you can live with, often something better than the company recommendation, and it makes the customer feel like they are in control. Feeling in control makes customers happy. With that, the sale is closed. If they don't have a viable plan, we offered a small discount if they paid cash. That eats into the commission, but it almost always makes the sale.

If this doesn't seem to work for you, keep in mind that not everyone is a salesperson. Some people are order-takers and some are salespeople. As an employer you really want salespeople and you really want to keep them with you over time.

Selling takes a lot of blocking and tackling, but it is also mental competition. As you can probably tell, I'm a fierce competitor. I really hate to lose. One of my favorite sayings is "Second place is first loser!"

To get the competitive edge in the phonebook ad business, we needed to have the physical drive, but we needed the mental discipline to make it sharp. Once again, I drew on my experience in sports to help me sort it out.

I remember experiencing this sort of mental competition when I was at a track meet at Brigham Young University in tenth grade. A Japanese athlete from Notre Dame was an expert at getting into peoples' heads. Our event was the 100-yard dash and I was so nervous and excited that I kept going to the bathroom. Have you ever been that physically and mentally nervous? Obviously, I have. My time came, and I got into the starting blocks.

As they made the call to get ready this Japanese kid jumped the gun. He didn't go very far before slowing down and turning back. Moreover, on top of it all, he took his sweet time getting back to the blocks.

While he sauntered back, he locked eyes with each one of us, as if saying, "I'm gonna beat every one of you guys." Then I realized that he'd jumped the gun on purpose. He'd jumped the gun just to get into our heads. He must've felt that it would give him an edge coming off the blocks. And in a short-distance race like the 100-yard, as in sales, timing is everything.

He won the race. By my senior year, I learned to play the head game with my opponents through story telling. I could tell some mind blowing stories (still can!) and get into my opponents' heads.

In sales, you can take the physical approach and try to browbeat people into buying from you, but I can tell you that it doesn't work very well. Those early phonebook salesmen used the physical approach to wring money from their "customers." If they'd had any real competition, however, they never could have been successful. The real trick is to compete on a mental level. If I can make you beat yourself, I have you truly sold. All the physical power in the world can't accomplish that.

Even putting a gun to someone's head won't "sell" them; it'll only make them buy from you. There is a very distinct difference. Physical competition can often land a sale without actually selling the customer, meaning you have to do it again (and it will probably be harder) the next time around. If you can mentally compete, you can get customers to sell themselves. Customers that are sold on your product develop a sense of loyalty.

Sometimes, I had to get creative in my mental techniques, just like the Japanese track star. I found that in working with advertisers, when I didn't see any other way to close, it was worth taking the chance on jumping the gun. Sometimes I would have this stack of checks from the other businesses I'd sold to recently—often a potential client's competitors—and I would pull them out of my pocket and mutter something about how "these other people felt they couldn't do without this ad; I wonder what's different about your business" and then shove them back into my pocket.

The goal was to turn it around in a way that if this particular client didn't want to buy, I could then make him or her worry that customers were going to think the business had closed. That was part of the value of having an ad in the phonebook, letting people know you were still around. Not only did that ad last for a whole year, it reminded potential customers that the business still existed. So I would try to get the client to see that if his ad was not in my book, people would think the business had closed.

Most of the time this scare tactic worked. In one of my phonebooks, I had the ads from every attorney in town, except one. He just wouldn't bite no matter what I tried, so I left him out of the book. Just a few weeks after the phonebooks were distributed he began calling me, frantic, because he realized that my book had almost a 90 percent penetration in his market. He didn't have an ad in the book so people thought that he was no longer practicing. Experiences like that taught me that sometimes you need to use a little mental conditioning and get inside the customer's head because they really do need what you're selling, they just don't always know it.

In the attorney's defense, I really understood his reluctance to buy. For a long time attorneys and CPAs were prohibited from advertising. It was a sector of the business that was slow to come around to phonebook ads. Eventually, after the regulation change, attorneys and plumbers became the top advertisers. When you're working with businesses, the mental "getting in their heads" technique is far superior to the physical, "bullying" one.

So, people always ask me, "What makes you such a great salesman?" I tell them these three things:

1. The Process: Approach, Warm-Up, Qualifier, Presentation and Close.

2. Free and Double: dumpster diving to get free phone listings more than doubled my business efficiency and accuracy; borrowing phone books from the big guys was also free and enhanced by my business—albeit a bit risky.

3. Physical vs. Mental: you have to have the physical drive and determination to keep going. I told all my salespeople: "Count the "No's" you get, not the "Yes's." If you know it takes 200 "No's" to get 300 "Yes's" count the "No's." And find a way to get in their head, even if you have to jump the gun.

They are my sales models, and I've never found a need to develop another one because I can make just about any sale using those three techniques.

CHAPTER 9

EXPANSION AND CONTRACTION

I'M ALWAYS AMAZED WHEN I THINK about it: at the heights of our business, we had 100 percent market penetration in Wyoming, Utah, and Alaska. Every business got a phone book in those states. I couldn't do that everywhere—between cost and competition—but I managed to get it done there, and I'm proud of that fact.

I remember when we were breaking into the Wyoming market. I walked into the phone company office in Pinedale, Wyoming, and cockily announced that I was there to sell ads in the new phone directories and that I would be taking away that part of their business. The manager didn't waste any time. He got his girls busy on the phones calling everyone in town and telling them that there were crooks in town to steal their money. I could not have paid for better advertising because now everybody knew who I was!

Unfortunately, I couldn't get anyone to listen to me, even though they did know I was coming and who I was.

The situation was not in my favor and was something very hard to overcome. It took me three years to do it, but businesses in the community eventually realized that I was not a crook and it was the local phone company they needed to be worried about. And, I learned from my mistake. If something doesn't work, don't do it again. Don't do the same dumb thing over and over. I learned then that it was much easier to avoid the local phone company and just start advertising my presence. In future cases I would just contact the businesses directly, kind of like a cold-call. I found that if I had the chance to tell my story myself and not have to battle the prejudiced stories of others, businesses would buy from me every time.

In the early days, when I was establishing offices all over the country, I quickly discovered that I needed a lot of fresh talent for my sales team; I couldn't do it all on my own. It was hard to find any veterans of the phonebook ad sales industry so I had to train them.

One of the most reliable sources I found was the pool of young men who were recently returned missionaries for The Church of Jesus Christ of Latter-day Saints. These guys had learned how to use a phonebook to find contacts on their missions, so they knew the product. They were also experienced in door-to-door contacting in an attempt to teach messages about their church; so, in a way, they knew how to "sell" something.

While they were serving their church, they worked in pairs, so I kept that pattern. I would send them to different areas throughout the U.S. in pairs, and if they would see the need for a local yellow pages in an area, I instructed them to start selling.

I quickly ran into a small problem, however. The problem with returned missionaries was that on their missions they had learned many valuable skills—like how to live off $100 a month, starve, and be content. This seems like a great quality on the surface, but it's a really bad quality in a salesperson.

When these guys got their first paycheck—sometimes as big as $1,000—they were bright enough to do the math and realize that they were much better off financially than they had been at any point in the preceding two years. Many of them were content with that first paycheck and stopped working as hard as they could have—all because they were no longer starving.

They were good salespeople to a point. They knew how to sell, but they lacked the intrinsic motivation to keep pushing harder. To be really good, my salespeople needed to always be hungry, always be driven. Even when they were making $10,000 a month in late-70s' dollars, I had to find a way to keep them hungry for more. I had to help them see how this could help them build wealth and not just acquire "things." I'll talk more about building wealth in the 10 Life Lessons a bit later. So, no jumping ahead please!

The limits of my salesforce weren't my only limits, however. I couldn't start up a new directory just anywhere—even in places that seemed perfect. I found that in many places there was some local guy—often someone in the chamber of commerce—who was already putting together a local phonebook. I quickly learned that there were a lot more independents than I ever imagined. For the most part, they were content to be little, so they didn't pose a direct threat. I, however, was not content to stay little.

In the 90s, there started to be a bit of a shift in the industry, one that had big implications for us little independents. Johnson Publishing, one of the larger independents, was getting out. They were already into their third-generation ownership and the new owners just wanted to be done. They had found a niche in the "local market" and had done well enough that they were able to sell that division of the company for $21 million. The independents had come in and revolutionized the industry, and now the phone companies were interested in buying up the companies that had a large, localized presence.

Unfortunately for me, I was scattered all over the country, which was both a blessing and a curse. The curse side obviously meant that I wasn't going to be getting any easy offers for my company. The blessing side was I had certain markets where there was little, if any, competition—like Alaska. And I was diversified in more ways than just geographically. I had recreational phonebooks, regional books, farming area books, mining area books, and more. I was very spread out. So I didn't get any offers during this time. Then again, when my offer did finally come, I took more money off the table than anybody else: a quarter of a billion dollars. But, more on that later. After all, timing is everything!

So, I wanted to grow. And I felt like now was the right time. Why? Because, to my way of thinking, we were a small to mid-size business—definitely on the smaller end. It's that place where you're too big to be a little company and too little to be a big company.

When you're in this danger zone you'll find bottlenecks all over the place. I decided to get out of there as fast as I could, and I either had to scale back to a small business again or push forward, quickly—otherwise I'd be eaten alive. The good news was, I knew there was a path forward. It wasn't easy, but everything up to this point had not been easy. We pushed forward.

One of the hardest things I dealt with was growing at the right speed. When you start out, you're nimble and reactive and you can change quickly to adapt to the business environment, but you're also broke—so broke that you worry about making payroll. Becoming a big business is a way to solve the payroll issue because you develop a pool of assets you can draw from to make ends meet over the short-term. However, being big isn't a perfect cure because you lose the agility and adaptability you enjoyed when you were smaller.

To make the jump, I needed to borrow money to get operations moving, but the interest rate was at a whopping 21.5 percent! If you borrow money at those rates, the banks own you and your company, even if you take out only the smallest of loans. At that interest rate, you need to really believe in what you're doing because you're betting everything on it. If you don't succeed —even if you just succeed slowly—the interest will eat you alive.

It was a big risk, but I believed we could do it.

I was already having some success by the time I went to the bank but I knew we needed more growth to get out of the new-business danger zone, so I "bet the farm" and borrowed $1 million. I couldn't get that kind of financing from the mainstream, main-street banks, so I went to one of those factoring institutions that charged 60 percent interest! I had to pay 5 percent, or $50,000, every month. It was a huge risk, but I had to do it.

The trick, I found, wasn't just watching what was coming in—making sure that I had enough revenue to meet the bank obligations. There were other considerations as well. My time living off the land and scraping by to save pennies taught me to watch both doors—the front and the back. I needed the financing to grow my revenues—to get more in the front door—but the tendency with growth is to allow more out the back door (or let more out in expenses) than what comes in the front.

Let me illustrate this for you.

The most valuable thing and the hardest to measure with sales, production, and delivery is time. Time really is money, and it can be stolen or wasted just like currency. Watching the back door means watching for time wasting. In my experience, 10 percent of your employees will never steal—ever. They will never take money, supplies, or even time from the company. These people are like gold. However, for every good employee, there's a bad one. I've also found that about 10 percent of employees are super thieves. They will steal anything and everything they can, from taking office supplies to skimming money off sales to taking excessive amounts of personal time while on the clock. Whenever possible, find these people and terminate them.

The other 80 percent of employees may take something if their own need is great enough. This is the "honest" salesman who makes a bad bet over the weekend and loses the money for his car payment. Then he up-sells a couple of accounts that week, submits them for less, and keeps the difference to cover his losses. Or the working mother who, realizing that school starts in a couple of days and she hasn't done the shopping for her kids, raids the supply closet for pens, pencils, paper, and notebooks. Neither of these people would have stolen under normal circumstances, but the need caught them off guard, and they saw an opportunity.

Camera-monitored time clocks, standardized (or even digitized) forms and reports, and office-supply controls help to rein in these kinds of losses, but people will still take things if nobody's looking. They aren't thinking about the impact to the company. That's one of the reasons you hire supervisors: to monitor time and supplies. Good supervisors will increase productivity at work more than they cost to employ them—they will pay for themselves. If they don't, then you need to find a different person, or a different technique, like the one I used in the following example.

Some of you reading this may find it amusing, while others of you might think it's disgusting, but at one point I noticed that our janitor would bring three extra bottles of water to the cooler around 4 p.m. every afternoon. I questioned him about it and he replied that there was always a line at quitting time for people getting water with their big gulp cups. I watched this for about a week and realized this water use was an extra dollar going out the back door every day, every week and every month. I came to the conclusion that it would be easy to stop this practice.

One day the janitor was not in so I proceeded to have one of the heavy water drinkers help me deliver water to the coolers. She took one bottle on a cart to one of the water coolers while I proceeded to fill another empty bottle from the back of the toilet tank with a large cup. She re-appeared just as I was about to finish filling the bottle and asked, "What are you doing?"

I replied I had noticed that we had increased our water usage by thousands of dollars a year because employees were taking water home. To reduce this cost I had been refilling the bottles for the last month from the back of the toilet tank because it was good clean water and can be dipped quicker than filling from the sink. As you can imagine, the grapevine is the fastest way to send a message. There were over 20 people telling human resources they just knew the water had a different taste and they were sure it had come from the toilet bowl itself. At any rate, we reduced our water consumption, and to my knowledge, nobody suffered from kidney stones. Like my earlier track opponent, I chose to play the mental game.

You really do have to watch the backdoor. Now, growth is a lot of fun when you've got the right people working with you. You can fit together seamlessly and make the most amazing things happen.

The "right" people might change over time, but that doesn't make the growth process any less exciting; it just means there might be a little heartache along the way.

Thankfully, our gamble worked. It wasn't easy, but after four months of putting everything back into paying off the loan, I was on top and I owned my company again. We were doing really well. Now, the question wasn't whether or not we could grow anymore. The real question was, "How big are we going to get?"

Things were going so well that I staffed up considerably. I even hired my wife and four sons. The business took so much of my time that I couldn't really think of another way to get more time with my family.

We now had nearly 600 employees so I also had to deal with the "equal opportunity employer" aspects of the law as well. Everyone in the company now had to have the same opportunities as everyone else. I didn't really have a problem with that. I had PhDs working for me that were making $40,000 to $50,000 a year in various types of positions, and college dropouts making far more than that. In fact, two of my sons didn't even graduate from high school and they were making close to $100,000 a year.

Times were finally good, and we were enjoying the fruits of our labors and growing fast! Before I realized it, we were a middle sized company.

Middle-sized businesses are too large for one person to run effectively yet too small to hire a bunch of management personnel. Not surprisingly, this middle tier is where most of the bankruptcies occur. It's a treacherous place, and you need to push through it as quickly as you can. Middle-sized companies tend to be those to suffer from bloat and waste with too much going out the back door.

I was in that stage for quite a while, certainly longer than I needed to be. My problem was that we had grown so fast that we were there before I knew it, and I didn't know what to do to get out. The good news was that we were listed in the top 100 fastest-growing companies in the United States in Inc. magazine.

Along with myself, others who appeared on that list were Steve Jobs and Steve Wozniak of Apple Computer and Alan Ashton of WordPerfect. I was in good company, to say the least. Then we went to number 228 the next year and number 444 the following year because we were getting too big for me to handle the company alone. I was okay with the growth figures, however (at least we were growing), but I didn't have the business experience in those transitional years during the early 80s.

We had some rough times ahead. Getting out of "No Man's Land" wasn't easy.

CHAPTER 10

THE RIGHT PEOPLE
ON THE BUS

Jim Collins coined the phrase in 2001 about getting the right people on the bus. And while I didn't know it at the time—back in the 80's and 90's—that is what I was actually doing.

Remember, my first focus was on the sales side. I was good at it and I could train others to be good at it, too. Sales weren't the only part of the business, however, and I had to keep the entire picture in mind or I would fail.

At first I was a little desperate, and I just hired people who were there, right alongside me – people I thought were a lot like me or whom I assumed I could train to be like me. I tried to get people I could push and motivate but that meant I had to periodically check up on them. Once I got the sales side of the business in order, I started to shift my focus to getting the other facets working smoothly.

I was finding that, as a business grows, there are inevitably positions that become necessary, people you didn't need before, but need going forward. One of the things I learned was that you must wait until the need is there before hiring for a new position. It did no good to have a distribution manager if I had nothing much to distribute – that was a waste of money. Worse yet, when I actually had books to distribute, my distribution manager had become used to sitting around doing nothing so he had a tendency to continue sitting around doing nothing. I therefore changed my strategy about hiring and my rule of thumb was to limp along until we were at risk of collapse, then hire the new person. Maybe that scares other people, but I was willing to put in the time and learn what I needed to do in order to keep the business going until we were really ready to hire new help.

Through those lean times and growing times, I did almost every job in the company. I'd be in a sales meeting in a three piece suit, end the meeting, shut the door, take off the jacket and go clean the bathrooms or do the accounting.

For example, I was not an accountant and I'm still not a numbers guy, but I could do graphs. I could model what we did in a particular year and make projections for the following year. More often than not, my projections looked like good growth. Imagine my surprise, when after the projected year arrived, I found we had usually exceeded the projections I had made. Like I said, I didn't have any formal training, and I don't think I was being too conservative in my projections, just realistic. Still, I was often pleasantly surprised at the end of any given year.

The sales team was my reason for learning how to put together a forecast. Having the projections gave them goals to shoot for. Even though I could no longer give them my undivided attention, as I had in the past, I continued to work with the team even after I shifted my focus to the publication side.

As things got moving along, I hired a CEO, a CFO, sales manager and distribution manager. These new specialists are purpose built, so they wear only one hat and only focus on that which is needed. For me, one of the harder parts about growing a company was shifting out of the entrepreneurial, start-up mindset where I had to do everything. Learning to let go and turn the responsibility for some aspect of the business to someone else is very tough. I knew that if I tried to run every aspect of a large company, I would burn myself out and the company as well. Having a management team in place meant I didn't need to be everywhere all the time, but it didn't let me off the hook entirely. I was still the CMO—Chief Motivation Officer.

I insisted that when my people came to work, they came to work. Everything else out there was BS (and that's not a bachelor of science), including all their problems at home or in their social life. My philosophy was that all that could stay where it belonged: outside of work. When my people came to work, they came to work. Nothing else mattered if they wanted to reap the benefits of being part of the company.

Of course, the sales team was always the toughest. Aside from the normal ups and downs, some lost motivation or had other problems. My experience was that about the bottom 25 percent of the sales team, the lower sellers, needed to be replaced regularly. Of course, we would only let someone go if they weren't meeting their goals, but they needed to know what was on the line at the outset. They needed to know that there was a standard to maintain, and those who couldn't maintain that standard would not be around for long.

The upside to letting people go like that was that the more replacements we had, the more chances we created to get people who will rise out of that 25 percent and be spectacular. As underperformers are cycled out, the incoming rookies get a chance to grow and become top performers.

The cycle kept the sales staff fresh and hungry. It's like a lake. If water flows in and flows out the other side, the water will stay good and it can support life. If you stop the water from flowing in, the lake will dry up and everything will die. If you stop the water from flowing out, something different happens. At first, the lake gets bigger. Then over time it starts to turn salty like the ocean. Eventually the salt will kill everything in the lake. That's how places like the Great Salt Lake in Utah are formed. You can't let your company become like the Great Salt Lake; you have to let people go and keep the flow moving to keep things fresh.

The salespeople who were at the top—those who made a terrific amount of money —were the individuals I called my "Brain Surgeons." I actually had ten of the top salespeople in all of the phone directory industry. These people made well over $100,000 per year. Some of them made as much as $250,000 a year. They lived and breathed sales as a way of life. They understood what I wanted and how I got it. They were the type of people I was looking for, and I held on to them when I found them.

We got to the point where we would have a week-long sales conference every year and training each spring. As my own responsibilities increased, I started bringing in big-name professionals to teach the sales force. Those conferences were worth every penny. Then, one day each year, we would bring in the entire company—sort of a "state of the business" meeting—and share numbers and goals.

I can't emphasize enough how important it was to share the numbers. It's always been my philosophy that every employee had the right to know how the company was doing—to know how much danger we were in or how good we were doing. Sure, during the rough times, some probably abandoned ship because of it, but most were loyal and stayed strong. Seeing the numbers helped them focus on what was important; it helped them keep their eye on the ball. Again, I have never been the numbers guy, but this new technique of sharing helped everyone understand and kept our team together.

As we grew, we attracted talent from some of our competitors and gained their inside knowledge. We started to look at the business models of our competition. If somebody else could do something for less money than we could, we needed to know where, why, and how. If we couldn't replicate the cheaper procedure in our company, we needed to outsource. If we could develop an even cheaper way of doing something, we instituted it. Once we got the whole company working behind that idea the profits really began to roll in.

We became such a profitable company because everyone was on board to do what we did and be the best anywhere at doing it. We had the whole company watching the back door for waste and working hard to bring more in through the front door. It was a good time to be in the yellow pages business.

Besides being the Chief Motivation Officer, I was also the CTO—the Chief Talent Officer. I was always on the hunt for good people. If I heard of a guy in New York City or Chicago or anywhere else, and he was the best salesman in that area, I was on a plane after him. That's how I got some of my best people. I had a bulletproof method for them to make money. Those who took the time to see that method soon realized that they could do better with me than with the position they currently held wherever they were. I got a lot of my top talent hunting them down and recruiting them.

Of course, the more people you have, the more people you have to pay. At one time I had 350 sales people working for me, and my printer had 150 working for him. I was always worried if I was going to make payroll. It was a big stress to me to have so many people counting on me to make that payroll. I didn't want to be the one to let anyone down. I paid the salespeople every week and everybody else every two weeks. Then, as soon as payroll was made, it would be time to start all over again. Everything was going so well—too well, as it turned out.

CHAPTER 11

TOO GOOD TO BE TRUE

A S THE BUSINESS GREW, NEW PROBLEMS began to beset me. At one point we hadn't been able to pay a printer on time so they held some phonebooks hostage in their warehouse. That opened up my territory to someone else and they moved in on my market in Oregon. I never could recoup that market so the printer and I sued each other. Nothing happened for three years until he got a judgment against me. I didn't have any more money to pay the judgment than I did to pay the original printing bill so the guy pulled up with a moving van and started hauling things away. I wasn't about to just sit by and let him dismantle my company so I went to my attorney and he told me the only solution was a Chapter 11 bankruptcy, then he handed me the papers.

Around this same time, unbeknownst to me, my wife started taking money out of the company, while saying the whole time "we have enough." My CFO warned me that if I did a joint tax return, which we routinely did at the time, and there were problems that both of us would be liable.

I owed this printer $153,000—money I would have had if he would release my books so that I could collect the ad revenue, or if my wife had not pulled $98,000 from the company without my knowledge. I told the printer, with the sheriff present, that I was filing a Chapter 11 and once I had it registered, which would be soon, he would have to put everything back in my building so he might as well stop and wait to see how the courts disbursed things. Alternatively, I offered him the $98,000 that my wife had taken, in cash, right then if he'd consider the debt paid in full. He did the smart thing and took the $98,000. That experience enlightened me to the fact that money was leaving the company without me knowing about it and got me thinking about what I needed to do.

Changes in life come at you fast, especially when the kids grow up while you have become a workaholic. It happened to me, and I've seen it happen to lots of other people. Starting your own business and making it flourish is a time-consuming, labor-intensive task. It is also a very lonely task. And remember, I don't mind being alone. I'm sure it's possible to have a family and run a business, but I hadn't quite figured out that balance. Finding out that my wife was taking money out of the company without my knowledge was a wake-up call.

Shortly after that incident, I went to a conference sponsored by Inc. magazine. At the conference, Dr. Ichak Adizes spoke about growing a company to its prime. There were more than 300 of us there for his lecture, but I felt like he was speaking directly to me; he was detailing my issues and explaining why they were happening, right there in front of everyone else. He never named me or my company, but I was sure he'd been sitting in on management meetings and shadowing my company for years. How else could he have known my problems so well, so specifically?

Turns out I was just one of many having the same problems, and Dr. Adizes had studied companies at my stage of growth. When an entrepreneur starts a company, he can do everything only to the best of his own abilities—meaning he doesn't do everything the best way possible. This shortcoming is, of course, based on a lack of knowledge on the part of the entrepreneur, not a lack of will or desire. Still, there is always somebody who can do something better than the entrepreneur, be it accounting or management or hiring. People—even entrepreneurs—instinctively know this and seek out people to shore up their weaknesses.

I recognized this and that's why I built my management team. So, where was my problem?

According to Dr. Adizes, as the company grows, the entrepreneur tries to maintain control over everything. When other people begin to have input and shape the evolution of the company, this often scares the entrepreneur, who feels like he's losing control, so he says, "That's the wrong way!" (because it's not his way) and the company begins to de-evolve.

This power struggle works like a rollercoaster—the company is doing nothing but going up and down, up and down. Obviously, this is not healthy and many will collapse from the stress of it. Dr. Adizes actually mentioned that when he comes in to help a company in this situation, they often have to help either a business partner or the entrepreneur go through a "divorce." Sometimes it's a divorce from a certain idea, sometimes it's a divorce from the company; usually it's a divorce between the partners of the company—too many chiefs, not enough braves. In any case, only through that divorce can the company make it to the next level.

In my case, the idea of a divorce was starting to look a little more literal. And how could it be any other way? Who were my partners? Most of the stock in my company was in my name. I'd given some minority stakes to some different people, especially those in my management circle, but I owned the thing.

Now, in addition, there was trouble between my wife and me. I now knew she had been taking money—how else could she get $98,000 in cash? But I didn't know if that's all that had been going on. Was there more to it? Was this something that had been going on for years? Or was it more recent and sudden? All I had were questions and I couldn't seem to get the answers.

When a partnership flourishes—be it marriage or business— everything gets discussed. In our partnership, nothing was getting discussed. What should that have told me? At that time I wasn't so much concerned about what got discussed and what didn't; I was more concerned about dishonesty. I can handle a lot of hardship and deprivation—I've lived off the back of a horse for six weeks at a time— but where I have trouble in my world is when someone outright lies to me, so much so that one of the first things I asked my current CFO when I first hired him was, "Are you going to steal from me? Don't steal from me. If you need it, ask me, and I'll give it to you, but don't steal." I know he hasn't, and I know he won't.

So, after I realized my wife was being dishonest and stealing from the company, we separated. We'd been married for 30 years, but I started sleeping upstairs and she started sleeping downstairs. We were technically still living in the same house, but we might as well have been on opposite sides of the country. Obviously, there were some issues on her side of the relationship, things going on that I didn't know about; otherwise she wouldn't have taken money out of the company without letting me know.

All I could dwell on was that it was all my fault. Maybe, if I had just been around more this wouldn't have happened.

But the past was in the past and the thought in my mind at that point was that I was living with a person I no longer knew. We had grown up together but we were like strangers on the street. It wasn't working in the company either because my boys were all leaning her way, probably because I'd been gone so much when they were younger. It just wasn't working out the way it was supposed to. This was a very painful time for me.

All along I had operated under the idea that the harder I worked the more money we would have. I'd grown up with nothing and I wanted my own family to have all the things I didn't have. And when I say "things," I wasn't talking about a bunch of toys. I'm talking about security, about peace of mind and the opportunity to give back to the world.

But now, here I was. The boys were all married and my wife was buying them each a new truck every year. The money was going to toys and goodies and not staying in the business to help it run. Where had I gone wrong? Where was my blind spot?

The golden goose was dying, and I felt like I was the one who let the arrow fly.

CHAPTER 12

THE WORLD FALLS APART

I WAS IN MY MID-40S DURING THE recession of the early 80s when my marriage finally fell apart. As I said, at that point, I more or less had two marriages: one to my high-school sweetheart and the other to my employees. I should have realized early that time couldn't heal all wounds—too much damage had already been done—but I was stubborn. I thought that time would turn the marriage around, but after nine years of dancing around the issue, it hadn't. Finally, it was time to call a spade a spade and realize that my high school sweetheart, who had been through the good times and the bad with me and who had raised our children, was gone.

When you look at the life cycles of men and women, there are "crazy times" for both. Unfortunately, in a marriage, crazy moments for one spouse don't necessarily coincide with the other. This constant bit of back-and-forth overlap as two people try to make things work can, in hindsight, make it appear to the marriage partners that there has always been something wrong between them. In truth, marriage is full of problems, that's just how it goes—even good marriages have plenty of problems. During my crazy times I never went out and bought a Porsche or anything—that wasn't my thing. I was, however, away a lot. I was constantly on the road and I liked to take trips for fun, too. My love of the outdoors never left me. It still hasn't. For my wife, one of her crazy times in life hit right around the same time she had a major surgery and then, again, shortly after her mother died. I was so busy I didn't take enough time for her. In any case, we had each changed enough that I woke up one day and realized that I no longer knew the woman I had married.

She probably didn't really know me either. So we separated.

I had a bunch of friends and employees at that time. From those ranks came several unattached women. They had reasons for being unattached. There was a reason I was also unattached. This did not make for a good situation. Whether or not they realized it, most women are attracted to money and power. I'd had neither when I got married the first time but I had both now and I was attracting the wrong kind of women. That kind of focus on money is not what you want to base a marriage on.

Through this whole marital upset, I was clinging to the business for all I was worth. After all, it was all I had. I didn't know anything else. Dr. Adizes' lecture on entrepreneurs and partners was fresh in my mind. I was realizing that my way was that of the entrepreneur—the idea man. I only knew how to do things to the best of my own abilities. Once I felt like I'd gotten something "right," I didn't feel a need to keep working to make it better. My marriage was the same way: I'd felt my marriage was "right," so I hadn't worked as hard to make it better.

As I went along in my marriage and building my company, with my dreamer mentality, I was like a small-town farmer. I didn't want all the farms in the neighborhood. I just wanted the one next to mine—the one where I expand and grow. Of course, as you grow, expand, and acquire, you soon realize that all the farms become "next to you" at some point. You start to lose track of what you already have as you look for the next great deal. That's why you've got to keep an eye on the back door. You have to keep an eye on maintaining what you have, both at home and at work or you'll end up like a person trying to fill a bucket that has a hole in the bottom.

I had around 700 employees by the time the divorce was in its final stages. Five different women who worked in my office discovered that there was trouble at home and all began to make a play for me. That helped my ego immensely at a time when I was really down. I didn't realize that they were really just attracted to my money and power. For a while—and this will make you laugh—I thought I was just that good-looking.

But I wasn't, and what I did was work my tail off. The business needed me, and it was uncomfortable to go home, so why not stay and work some more? The attention of those women really only served to compound the existing problems and put me in the crosshairs.

The church I belonged to at the time has very strict standards regarding the interactions between men and women—especially the level of physical interaction. Having all those women after me at the office convinced someone that I had broken those standards. When church leadership learned of it, they called me in for what's called a church council. In reality, it was more like a court, and the local leadership had to decide whether or not I would be able to maintain my membership.

They asked me a lot of questions about what had happened between my wife and me, but I wouldn't say anything. Even after the awful time we'd had recently, we'd still had decades of good times together. I wasn't about to betray her and the memory of our family by saying anything negative. I would not talk badly about her; we hadn't been living together for some time, but that didn't mean I didn't care. I still loved her on some level, I just knew we weren't meant to be anymore.

I refused to make a comment.

The leadership warned me that if I didn't defend myself, they would excommunicate me. I told them that there was no story coming out of me. So, I was severed from the church. My membership in the church—something I'd had since childhood—had now been taken away, too.

In a lot of respects, my whole world had been pulled away like a rug from beneath my feet. I felt betrayed. As a Jaycee, I learned the value of a holistic and balanced life, which included the spiritual side. I had done nothing wrong; nevertheless, I was denied the association of the spiritual side of my life. What was I to do? I picked myself up and moved forward.

CHAPTER 13

PICKING MYSELF UP AGAIN

Enter Debbie. During these troubling times, one of my friends invited me on a double date—a fishing trip. Debbie was there. We developed a connection and I think she took a liking to me—I certainly liked her. She looked great, spoke well, handled herself well, and liked to go hunting and camping with me—which suited me to a "T." It didn't take long before we were an item. She began to work side-by-side with me. With her, I knew exactly where I stood. It was refreshing after so many years of wondering what was going on behind the scenes.

While I can be a little bit wishy-washy at times, Debbie can call a spade a spade almost at first glance—and she's not afraid to do it. Usually, she uses that gift to tell you how to make yourself a little brighter. If I know that a person is angry with me, I usually have to take some time to think through things and eventually see the way to straighten myself out. Debbie can always pinpoint the issue right away. It is a gift I needed desperately at that time on a personal level and a business level. I wanted to have her nearby.

She became the right person for the sales-management seat on my bus in just the nick of time. I had been a pushover at times with a lot of my sales people. I'd say things like, "You do that one more time and you're gone." Of course, if they did it one more time, I didn't actually fire them, I just warned them again. I was always ready to give them another chance. Then there'd be another chance, and maybe even another. It was that government-worker mentality that I couldn't quite shake. Besides, these people had been with me through so much; I couldn't just let them go now.

But Debbie applied the rules of baseball. You could make a mistake once; that was just human. If you made that same mistake again, she would train and educate you. She figured it might have been her fault that you weren't taught well enough. Third time—you were gone. The sales force straightened up with her in charge. She was a true equal-opportunity employer. It didn't matter if a person was the top salesperson in the company. If that person couldn't straighten up, Debbie would send them packing. It didn't matter where anyone was on the scale of best to worst; they shaped up or she shipped them out.

Truthfully, after some of the mistakes I'd made, I'm lucky she didn't send me packing!

The whole process of severing those ties with my first wife took nine years—nine years of unhappiness for everyone. It was during that time that I met Debbie, May of 1985. She had been working for a bank I dealt with. Eventually, she came to work for me, but things got too hot in the kitchen—both personally and in the business—so she went back to work for the bank. This was the one time she did send me packing, and for good reason.

It took some pretty clever convincing to get her to come back, but she finally did.

At that time, she already had two daughters, ages 3 and 6. She was a relatively happy camper in her situation after divorcing her husband of nine years. I was the father figure in that little family—even before we were married—because the biological father had chosen to remove himself from the picture. In some ways, I looked at it as a second chance for missing so much when my own children were growing up. I loved those girls then and love them now as if they are my own. Eventually, we moved in together and then got married a few years after that on February 1, 1997.

Debbie is perfect for me, and I love her to death. We can attend big social functions together and then go camping and climbing together. She fits in both worlds, effortlessly. She is a very powerful woman. I tell everybody that the reason I married her was because I couldn't afford to let anyone else have her. We balance each other. We make up for—well, she makes up for my deficiencies.

After we got married, she came back to Phone Directories Company as the vice president of sales. She really was excellent and exactly what we needed. She was a people person who still knew how and when to say "No." I was a people person, but I did not know (and I still don't know!) how to say "No." I was a pushover sometimes, and she called me on it right away.

I guess I had too much sympathy for the "salesman and his plight" after all those years doing the sales myself. She had mercy, but she also had justice. She straightened me out, then we straightened out the company, and then things went really well. Even just this "slight" change was enough to take the company to another level. We became a mega-company in very little time, a testament to the idea that you need the right people in the right seats on your bus.

Throughout this period, I attended my church occasionally—even though I had been excommunicated—but I wasn't really involved for about 15 years. Near the end of my inactive period, Debbie and I had a couple of church members who would come and visit us regularly to share messages about church teachings. These members—called Home Teachers—were great. They were always checking on us and making sure that things were going well, even though I wasn't technically a member of the church anymore. They visited us regularly for about three years before one of them asked me, "How come you've never come back to the church?"

I replied, "Well, nobody ever asked that closing question before, and I didn't want to embarrass anybody."

Debbie and I were both excommunicated from the LDS Church when we moved in together. We didn't have anything against the LDS

Church, really, but we had just never taken the time to repair the broken issues in our respective spiritual lives. Thanks to those Home Teachers, we both came back and now we've been sealed in the temple—one of the most sacred and important commitments Latter-day Saints can make.

CHAPTER 14

A GROUNDWORK FOR GROWTH

WITH DEBBIE ON BOARD, WE WERE READY to reach new heights. It was a struggle. We were facing bankruptcy and it took us six years to pull it out. By 1996, our lobbying in Congress had been instrumental in the creation of the Telecommunications Act. The benefit of this act was that the utility companies were now mandated to sell their listings at no more than 4 cents per listing. This was a huge win for us, the independents, because it meant we could afford "to buy" the listings, rather than "procuring" them through extravagant means like I had used in the early days of the business. However, you will be delighted to know that I am still a proficient and superb dumpster diver!

Additionally, the listings were to be provided to the independents on tape or disk or some other electronic, easy-to-access form. This was a second coup for us. It meant we wouldn't have to retype everything in order to work with the material. A lot of the utility companies refused, so Congress tripled the damages. Pretty soon, the utilities got the message that they were not protected or privileged any longer. The Information Age was in full swing, and Phone Directories Company was poised to ride the wave to the top.

As the computer industry made managing listings much easier, we independents started getting creative and putting our own unique types of numbers in our listings. These numbers would be given to businesses—say a pizza parlor—that wanted to track their phone calls.

We gave them a free ad in the yellow pages part of the directory in exchange for being able to track the number and type of calls. We used that information to determine the market and customer usage.

Then to add some icing to our already wonderful cake, telecommunications technology advanced enough to require new infrastructure. The utility companies began laying fiber optic cables in the ground, racing against one another to lay the foundation for the Internet and other data-transfer applications—and all the revenue that would come with it. Of course, fiber-optic cable isn't cheap—and neither is all the labor of digging trenches from one coast to the other. So, to gain the capital that the operation needed, the utilities started to sell off their highly profitable phone directory divisions to some of the independents.

It was like the skies had opened and the lucky breaks were flowing freely!

We began to grow the business in ways we couldn't have dreamed of 10 years prior. I brought in a new president and he was working well. We brought in a new CFO, Michael Bingham (not a relative). It was clear skies and smooth sailing, except that we needed more funding to continue to accelerate our growth. So we brought in a partnership with Seidler Equity, built by the same O'Malley family that purchased the Brooklyn Dodgers and took them from New York across the country to Los Angeles.

The deal was that they were to put up $15 million in soft money for the business with $5 million of hard money. Hard money is financing that the equity company gives directly. There is very little in terms of regulation around the hard-money lending industry, so the money is "easier" to get, but often comes with difficult terms or higher interest rates. Soft money is traditional lending, like from a bank, with well-regulated terms and more competitive interest rates.

The $5 million hard money from Robert Seidler came with stipulations and conditions a plenty. If we failed to meet as single one of them, he had the ability to take control of the company. We agreed and proceeded. He now owned a percentage of our company and had three years before he could opt out—or abandon his ownership stake. The soft money was supposed to come in as well.

It never did. Seidler never got that financing or he never gave it to us. Either way we didn't get the rest of the money we needed.

Seidler's idea was that we were going to level off the company and start milking the profit margin. He wanted to get rich and fat off of it—probably in an effort to dilute my level of control. I still held the majority of the stock. He said that the CFO and the president should have some ownership. His rationale was that they would be more connected to the company and work harder to make it run properly. I gave 10 percent to the president and a few percentage points to my CFO. But none of that was why I'd brought Seidler onboard in the first place. The utilities were putting their directories up for sale and I wanted to buy some.

After bringing in that $5 million, believing that an additional $15 million was coming, I spent $7 million acquiring some new companies. When the other $15 million didn't arrive, I had to find $2 million somewhere—it came out of my pocket.

Was it painful? You bet.

Was it worth it? Absolutely.

After that experience, I realized that I had to somehow get rid of the partnership with Seidler. The cash had been very welcome, but insufficient. What's more, the inactivity—the lack of involvement — was not welcome. He had basically bought into the company and now wanted to ride on our coat tails forever. I had to get rid of him somehow or he could drag the company down or even worse, take control.

CHAPTER 15

ONCE MORE INTO THE BREACH

OUT OF THE BLUE, IN 2005, I HAD AN OFFER come in to purchase some of our operations. The offer was $50 million for the Canadian operations. In Canada, I was the largest publisher of phone books. I had books from Victoria to Halifax. That offer got me thinking in a direction I had previously never gone. I had never really considered liquidating a chunk of the business. I'd had to sell bits and pieces here and there to pay the bills, but I'd never sold such a huge part of the company at one time.

It also got me thinking about what the company was really worth. I didn't mind selling—it would give me the capital to get rid of Seidler—but I was always looking to get the best deal, and I had no intention of letting part of my company go for less than it was worth. I talked with my president about it and he thought we should run it through an auction, so we hired Dave Dunn from Signal Hill out of Baltimore.

We sent 125 letters to different entities and received 60 responses. From those, we took the top 10 to the next round. Each of the offers in that round had to top $55 million—the top bid from the first round. It was interesting to me that the first company, whose offer was $50 million, was not even in the last round, and they had given me the idea. When they realized they'd been left out of the second round they came up to $56 million, so we let them back in and had 11 companies bidding for the option to buy the Canadian branch of Phone Directories

Company. One of the bidding companies happened to be the major telecommunications company for the Mountain West, U.S. West. However, an offer for their company came up at the same time and they backed out, so we ended up with 10 bidders.

The auction process began in earnest, and the Canadian part of the business ended up being sold for $81 million. Once I had the money, the next step was to get rid of Seidler. It cost me $14 million to force Seidler out a year earlier than his option date, but I was not going to give him the chance to stay longer. With him gone and plenty of money left, I decided it would be nice to share a little of that success around the company.

I gave my president $10 million for a job very well done. That turned out to be a mistake. Just as I had seen in the early days of hiring LDS returned missionaries and their change in behavior when earning big checks, I saw a change in my president immediately. His feet went up on the desk and he became worthless. As great as he had been up through the sale, he was that much more worthless afterwards. I had rid the company of Seidler so I fired my president, too.

We lost about a third of our company with the Canadian sale, including a number of talented salespeople. Without missing a beat, Debbie went to work in retraining the sales force to up the revenues. She did excellent work, and we moved up and took on some other companies. Within a year of the Canadian sale, the company that had purchased that arm from us—HM Capital, out of Dallas—was interested in buying our U.S. operations as well.

Only, I didn't want to sell. It was my company and I wasn't quite ready to part with it. HM Capital explained that the Canadian purchase was so great for them that they wanted to buy the U.S. business, too. I told them that I didn't want to sell until 2010, when the tax laws were going to change and I was planning on retiring. They asked me, "What if it was already 2010? What would the selling price be?" I told them that it would be worth at least $150 million by then. They reiterated that Canada had been good and that they would look at the numbers.

They came back with their offer. I decided, then and there, in 2007, to sell. After all, why work three more years to get the same price I could get right then? So, I sold the company at 20 times the EBITA (earnings before interest, taxes and amortization) for $150 million. They, of course, immediately fired me, but I kept ownership with a $10 million stake.

Of course the U.S. operations were very different than Canada, so HM Capital ended up selling the Canadian business for $350 million. Goldman Sachs were the big money people who financed the HM Capital purchase. We closed right before the financial markets collapsed in 2007 and Lehman Brothers was allowed to die. If we had waited two weeks it never would have gone through, because the capital wouldn't have existed. Again, I maintain that timing is everything. Take the opportunity when it comes to you, or you're likely to lose it forever.

I think luck may have had something to do with it as well.

WHAT TO DO NEXT

WHAT NOBODY TELLS YOU, before you sell a business, is that the world changes on the other side. First of all, you cash out all of that net worth which, until you sold the business, was just a set of numbers on a page. It's different to look at the "estimated value" of your company in some analyst's report versus looking at that number in your bank account. The other thing is that you've poured heart and soul into building that business for so long that you kind of find yourself lost. You have plenty of money and nothing to do. That's a dangerous combination if you plan to keep any of your money.

So, I got moving again.

I placed $24 million in a fund. I donated another $15 million to Utah State University. They built an extension to the university in Vernal, Utah, called the Bingham Entrepreneur, Energy, and Research Center. USU and the community, over seven years, leveraged that $15 million into nearly $100 million of community development

I sent another $1 million to Utah Valley University. President Matthew Holland came to me and told me that if I could donate half the money he could raise additional funds from the legislature to for a new science building. He also told me that they were the biggest university in the state of Utah—as measured by number of students—but they had no room to put them. Education is important to me, so I wanted to help out.

If you can conceive it, you can achieve it.

The early years before the U.S. entered World War II.

A young boy learning about life just before the accident.

Uintah High School, just before graduation.

Working as a conservation officer in the Salmon River country while employed by Idaho Fish and Game.

For 1969

20th DSA WINNER . . . Marc Bingham, left, accepts Distinguished Service award presented by Price Junior Chamber of Commerce. Making presentation is Toy Atwood, Price City councilman and previous DSA winner. S-A Photo

Receiving the Distinguished Service Award from the Jaycees.

President of the Jaycees, in Price, Utah.

Pack trip in the High Uintas.

Marc bags a Marco Polo sheep in Kyrgystan.

Debbie's Desert Bighorn Sheep taken in Southern Utah.

Leadership team at Phone Directories Company.

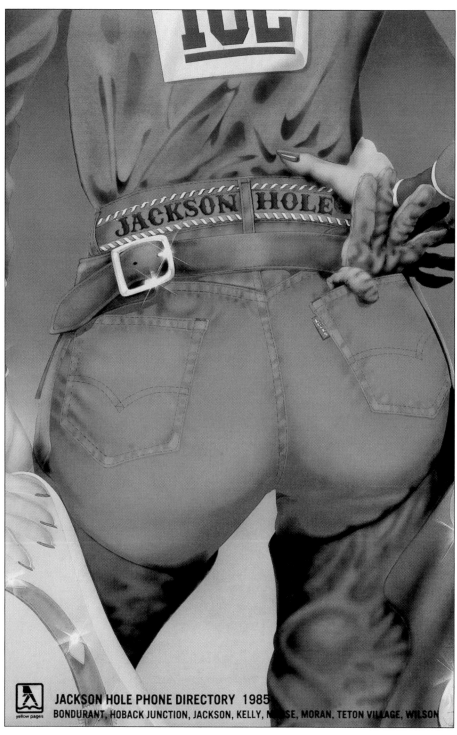

The controversial phone directory cover that was later banned by the city of Jackson Hole, Wyoming, and then profiled in the February 1986, issue of Playboy Magazine.

Marc gets his Transcaspian Sheep in Turkmenistan.

Touring Xining While on a Blue Sheep hunt in China.

*The Bingham Entrepreneur and Energy Research Center
at Utah State University Vernal, Utah.*

Marc and Debbie after the sale of Phone Directories Company.

Roots of Knowledge, stained glass mural at Utah Valley University Library, Orem, Utah, made possible by a donation from the Binghams.

Visiting with former Vice President Dick Cheney.

In Jerusalem with the Dome of the Rock shrine in background.

Fishing in Prince William Sound, Alaska.

At Full Curl Sheep Camp in British Columbia.

At the 2017 inauguration of President Donald J. Trump in Washington, D.C.

With President Donald J. Trump.

Marc and Debbie with Utah Governor Gary R. Herbert and First Lady Jeanette Herbert at the Butterfly Biosphere.

Mount Vernon, Virginia.

Nuremburg, Germany.

*Marc and Debbie hosting Donald Trump, Jr. and former
Secretary of the Interior, Ryan Zinke.*

I also couldn't stay away from wildlife. Because of all that time as a wildlife manager I decided to buy a wilderness unit called the Arctic Red River Outfitters in the Northwest Territory of Canada. Then I turned around and donated it to the sportsmen with one condition: 10 percent of all the expeditions or excursions must be given away to people who could not usually afford such a trip or experience. I wanted to set something up to help people enjoy the wilderness who wouldn't normally have that chance (such as veterans through the Wounded Warriors project, for instance). I've received many letters of appreciation from people who have been able to enjoy an amazing outdoor experience because of these donated expeditions.

Then I was diagnosed with prostate cancer. I endured surgery and radiation, which helped for a couple more years, but still didn't cure me. That's when I found the University of Denver Hospital. They put me on hormones, that have done some other, non-dangerous-but-equally-unattractive things to my body. Even with those unwanted side effects my cancer is now under control.

They really took care of me. So, I donated $1.5 million to what became the Bingham Cancer Research Center at the hospital. The stipulation with the University of Denver is that the money is to be used for research and to help people who can't afford treatment. It's already working. I just sent somebody there during the course of writing this book and he and his doctor have already called back with good news.

One of the more important things Debbie and I did was to set up a fund for the education of our grandkids. Education is extremely important to us and we wanted to make sure they all have that opportunity. We put about $4 million into that endeavor. It's good for books and tuition, and they only have to maintain a C average to qualify, which is not too hard to do in today's world.

If they don't maintain the average, they have to pay back to the fund. I had one granddaughter comment that I could afford to send her to college and pay all the expenses, not just tuition and books. I then said to her, "Yes, but I don't take those kinds of gambles." If I were going to gamble, I would go down to Vegas and watch the wheel hit red or black three or four consecutive times; then I would bet on the opposite. Paying an entire education for someone is like putting all that money on one number of the roulette wheel. I'd be betting on one person, and I won't do that.

For my six children, four boys and two girls, I paid off their home mortgages. Then I took a lien back and told them that every year they were to pay me the interest accrued on the loan and I would take care of their property taxes. It lets them have a tax credit and gives me a place to park some of my net worth. Upon reaching age 55, the lien on their homes will end and the houses will revert back to them. I have stipulated, however, that if one of them happens to go through a divorce, he or she owes me everything I have paid on their mortgage, but their equity is theirs to divide with their spouse. I've done divorce and I want them to have an incentive not to follow in my footsteps.

CHAPTER 17

HAVING FUN

A S THE ADAGE GOES, "work hard or play hard, don't just sit around." I worked hard for lots of years—and continue to work hard now—so I've earned my chance to play hard.

Since slowing down in 2007, I have spent a great deal of time outdoors, which is one of my greatest passions. As a hunter and wildlife enthusiast I have taken the challenge of hunting down rare animals from all over the world. I am one of probably only about 100 people on earth who has found what they call the "World Slam," which is 12 different species of sheep out of the 48 recognized possible species worldwide.

Debbie was the first woman in the state of Utah, and 42nd in the world, to get the "Grand Slam." That honor consists of hunting down these four species of North American Sheep: the Dahl's Sheep (from Alaska), the Stone's Sheep, the Rocky Mountain Bighorn, and the Desert Bighorn. We built a "mountain" setting inside our home in Vernal, Utah, so we'd have a place to display the fully mounted bodies of our collectively hunted 22 different sheep.

I've had the chance to participate in some of the most challenging sheep hunts in the world. To be the "Great White Hunter," for example, you need to acquire the Marco Polo Sheep, a species of the Argali Sheep named after the famous explorer. The reason why it is such a prize is that its native habitat is in the mountains of Asia, and you have to hunt it at between 15,000 and 20,000 feet in elevation.

Most of the people who hunt there are a little bit older than your average hunter, people more like me, and the altitude sickness can really get to you. It feels a lot like you have the flu and if you lay down to rest for a few hours, you die. There's a 10 percent hunter mortality rate, which is the odd attraction and extra challenge of hunting the Marco Polo. The danger lies not in the animal itself, but in the environment of the hunt. It is actually a rather plentiful sheep, if you can brave the altitude to find them.

In addition, I have also had the opportunity to acquire the rare Mongolian sheep called Altay Argali. It is extremely uncommon and, therefore, expensive to hunt. The hunt is very strictly controlled because there are so few of the sheep in the wild. They have to control the trade and only let a certain number be culled every year or the species will go extinct. Big bucks for big bucks, I guess you could say.

One of the most exciting hunting experiences for me was discovering that I was hunting in the same area as one of the world's foremost sheep hunters, Jack O'Connor. O'Connor was once a writer for Outdoor magazine and its shooting editor for 31 years. At one point on this hunt, I crawled under a rock overhang to get out of the weather. There I found a .270 Winchester shell on the floor, which was Jack's signature shell and gun. I don't know if it was his shell, but it was fun to think that perhaps it was and to know that I was in a place in which he may have hunted.

CHAPTER 18

DIAMONDS IN THE ROUGH

Once Debbie and I got some of the hunting and fishing taken care of, we got bored. Really. Truthfully. I am a Type A personality and could not sit home and watch TV or sit around and count my money. Believe it or not, I actually got bored sorting nuts and bolts in my yard sale treasure yard. We both needed a challenge. And it was a big challenge. The recession was in full swing and we were committed.

We had asked our CFO, Michael Bingham, and few other key people we couldn't do without, and formed Blue Diamond Capital, a family office—which currently has 82 active projects.

When we started, one of our first purchases was Wheeler Park in Heber City, UT. We worked the deal and had the property entitled for paper lots. We had a three phases of development and we did all the improvements on the first phase. The first phase sold out to Desert Point and Richmond America. As the recession worsened, Desert Point took out bankruptcy and Richmond America came to a screeching halt. In the meantime, we took the risk of improving the other two phases.

The economy was tanking. People and companies were going down, life savings were lost. I lost $30 million on the stock market, but, fortunately, had plenty of cash on-hand and I had made some good purchases.

We decided that paper lots could not be sold. So we decided to build homes on the lots and sell them. We engaged four builders to build four homes each. One builder's group sold out immediately. The other three struggled.

We got to know that home building company. It was Edge Homes. They were successful because they built a quality product and had a great sales team. Their biggest drawback was that they were spending thousands of dollars working through appraisals and bank financing. We struck a deal with them and became their bank.

What was exciting for me was that we started building a team. I'm really good at building the team. After seven years of growing the team and company, Edge Homes became the second largest homebuilder in the state of Utah. Prior to 2013, we had been building about 40 homes a year. By May of 2013, however, we ramped things up and had built 750 homes since the first of that year. At one point, we surpassed Ivory Homes, which had been Utah's premier home builder for two decades.

My role in the company was really just to act like the bank. One of my friends remarked recently that EDGE Homes must be a really great company. I told him it is, and largely because of a fantastic younger management team, all aged between 35 and 50. I love to associate with young blood because of their energy. They keep me feeling young, and at age 78, that's not easy to do.

Why did I like EDGE Homes? I love mentoring and it gives me the opportunity to do so. I have discovered over time that the people I love to associate with are, in a way, like children—eager and full of energy and drive—if I can teach them to avoid the mistakes I made, I can help contribute to their ultimate success. I try to help them avoid those difficult times I experienced, or, if they are already going through them, I try to direct them to better paths. Where I had to dig out and up to get to the top, I can show them more effective ways to go through that digging out.

In the last year we owned Edge Homes, we built and sold 1600 homes. We put the company up for sale and it was purchased by Sumitomo Forestry for $192 million.

You'd think after all the headache I went through in my partnership with Seidler at Phone Directories Company that we would hate each other. That's not the case at all. We are still great friends and have mutual investments and ownership in several companies.

Emergency Essentials, an emergency preparedness store in Utah, is one of them. Another of our investments is Sportsman's Warehouse, America's Premier Outfitter. The previous owner started having some financial trouble so I loaned him some money, but he entered bankruptcy anyway. Seidler and I bought it and brought it out of bankruptcy. I put about $1 million into it and I've been blessed to get $15 million back as a publicly traded company. I'd say that's not a bad return on investment really, but it's still down on list of accomplishments I've managed since retirement.

Remember the $30 million we lost in the recession with Merrill Lynch? Well, we stayed the course while many people bailed out. To date, we have made our $30 million back and more during the rebound. "You gotta know when to hold 'em and when to fold 'em."

We haven't stop dreaming, working and expanding. We are heavy into real estate development. We have partnered in over 40 hotels (mostly Marriot and Hyatt), we've also partnered in Visionary Homes in Logan, UT, and we are a principal (along with Clyde Companies and Utah's State Institutional Trust Lands) in 3500 acre master-planned community in St. George, UT called Desert Color.

Truly exciting times!

If there's one thing I've learned in slowing down, it's that money really does not buy happiness. I have made at least 10 people millionaires, and only two of them have maintained their fortune. The rest fell in love with the idea of their money and spent it all, which caused severe unhappiness and hardship for those individuals.

I've thought a great deal about those 10 people and the others than have done well with me and have lost much. I can't stop people from making mistakes, but I can advise them, encourage them, and mentor them. I think that if you can make it five years through the process of adjusting your thought process regarding money—without making disastrous personal, ethical or moral mistakes—you can endure to the end of any endeavor with which you may be involved.

That said, most people need a little mentoring to get through the change in the way they look at life. I would recommend that you seek advice from someone who's been there, not from someone who's about to leap off the cliff into the same endeavor. That way you can be counseled with, "I know about that – I've been there," and "I see what's going on." Remember, the wisdom that comes from these mentors can not only be antiseptic but inoculation, too: it repairs and protects.

One of the more successful theories I've developed is a way to cultivate wealth. It's a series of ten steps that I call "The Lessons of Life." During my time with Phone Directories Company, I set up a "Five Percent Club," telling people that they had to stay with me until "the end." We developed an exit strategy wherein we would take 5 percent of the sale price and share it among the people in that club who had endured with me to "to the end."

What we actually ended up doing was giving them their share in stock. It was easier to split up that way, and there were tax advantages, too. Unfortunately, as is true with any gift, some of the people thought it was great while others thought I should have given more. Over the years, I've kept in touch with most of those people and found that because it was a "gift," most of them wasted that money buying new cars, clothes, fancy meals and parties, vacations, or other toys—items of depreciating and temporary value—instead of investing it in their future. I feel a little guilty about how it turned out because it means I hadn't taught them the Life Lessons.

It's not every day that a person gets a payday or bonus of that size. It happens once, maybe twice in a lifetime. When it happens, there is a strong temptation to better your current, short-term situation, like most of my 5-percenters did. However, surprise money like that should go to something that will help secure your future. The unfortunate fact about money is that, whether it is easily won or hard won, it is always easily gone. Those who went through the money most quickly thought I should have given them more. That made me really sad; I had given them a gift and they were dissatisfied that somehow I hadn't given enough.

Most of those in the Five Percent Club did all right with their money. I had one guy, however, who told me that he still had every penny of the original bonus. He had invested it and was receiving some modest payoffs. Because of his diligence, I was able to show him a few ways to increase that income without a high risk on the input, or the principal. He learned my lessons quickly and is doing very well now.

That experience, and others, convinced me that I can take a person into the top 10 percent of the wealthiest people in America if they will follow my formula. I've been teaching that formula on a limited basis since about 2000, and I've found that following the 10 basic lessons that I am about to outline makes the road to self-actualization shorter. It's not any easier—it's never easy—but the time it takes to get there becomes less.

I'm still perfecting the process of teaching these 10 lessons, and I will probably continue to improve until I end up leaving this earth. I have 10 to 12 people going through it with me at any given time. I worry that only two out of the 12 will make it, because most of them say to themselves something like, "I'll get started tomorrow." Procrastination is the number one reason for the failure of anything.

My process is really all about making yourself the CFO of your own life and watching that back door. I have some advice about how to cut expenses and do without. If you can do without when you have little money, imagine what you can do without when you have a lot of money. Frugality keeps you on the millionaire track; people fail when they think they've "made it" and can start to spend what they've worked so hard to earn.

I'll share the short version of the 10 lessons here in hopes that some of you will understand them, apply them and become wealthy because of them. Best of luck, but remember that "luck" is just the intersection of knowledge, opportunity, and hard work. I've created my own good luck. I wish you the best in creating yours!

The
10 Life
Lessons

NET WORTH VS. WAGE

L ESSON 1 IS FAIRLY SHORT. We're going to plant an idea in your head and see how it grows. If you don't grasp this concept, the rest of the lessons won't help you much; so open your mind as you keep reading. Some of you will naturally understand this; for the rest of you, pay attention and focus on the concepts. No matter who you are, don't move on to Lesson 2 until you "get" Lesson 1.

We've all heard the expression that "the rich get richer, and the poor get poorer," but the truth is actually more frightening than that. In the past 50 years, the wealth gap between the richest one percent of Americans and the typical family has more than doubled. In 1962, the top one percent had about 125 times the net worth of the median household. By 2010, that difference had grown 288 times.

In other words, the rich are getting richer, but the poor aren't the only ones getting poorer; basically the middle class is also getting poorer. The net worth of the median household in America actually fell over the period of 1983 to 2010, dropping from $73,000 to $57,000. This is especially interesting when you consider the fact that the average wage rose over the same period.

Even after the financial woes of 2007 to 2009, people are typically making more now than people did in 1983 (or 1962). So, shouldn't people be getting wealthier since they are making more money?

Granted, things cost more now than they did back then, but shouldn't wealth at least have grown proportionately with increase of wages?

To answer that, we need to explore the difference between wages (income) and net worth. We also need to look at the difference between real wealth and how society today perceives wealth.

WEALTH IN AMERICA VIDEO

I highly recommend viewing a YouTube video that went viral some time ago. It does an excellent job of displaying, visually, the disparity between middle-class America and the super wealthy. Before I give you the link, let me just point out that I'm not showing this to you from a political standpoint. The maker of the video expresses some political bias (the comments express even more), and I am not going to turn this into a political discussion.

This book is about helping you develop the mindset that will drive you to wealth, not about trying to change your political ideology. But the message about money and wealth is clear, so it's worthy of viewing.

While you watch, pay attention to how the video distributes wealth and then uses that distribution to highlight the current problem in the American system of wealth retention. The lesson is not about trying to change that mechanism here but to learn to leverage it for your own advantage. Also remember that I'm not talking about wages or income; I'm talking about net worth:

http://www.youtube.com/watch?v=QPKKQnijnsM

(If, for some reason, the link doesn't work, try searching YouTube for "Wealth Inequality in America." It's a six minute video.)

What do you think? That video paints an interesting picture, doesn't it?

The thing the video fails to point out is that "fixing" wage distribution won't "fix" wealth distribution. There is a huge disparity in earnings, true, but the real problem is something else entirely: those low earners tend to want the same things that the superrich want—nice cars, nice electronics, nice houses, nice education, etc. What ends up happening is that these low earners spend their entire annual wage (and sometimes more) trying to get all the "stuff" that only the rich can afford. These "poor" people are trying to use their limited resources to buy happiness, and it's that mentality that prevents them from accumulating wealth and moving from the bottom 20 percent to the top 20 percent.

Wealth isn't about the wage you earn. Plenty of people get wealthy on limited wages, and plenty of people go bankrupt on extremely high wages. The key to becoming wealthy is to understand net worth and its importance and then work to increase your net worth regardless of your salary.

AVERAGE NET WORTH IN AMERICA

So let's define net worth. For our purposes, net worth is the total combined value of all your assets minus any liabilities. That's accounting-speak for the value of everything you own (houses, cars, bank accounts, stocks, etc.) minus any money you owe (credit cards, mortgages, auto loans, etc.). This is a fairly simple definition, but it makes it much easier to visualize your own net worth. All you need to do is total up the value of all your assets and then total up the cost of all your debts. Subtract your debts from your assets and you get your net worth.

Let's run through an example.

Joe owns his home, two cars, has some cash in the bank, and contributes to his 401k...occasionally. His home is worth $320,000; his cars are worth $8,000 and $19,000 respectively; he has about $7,500 in the bank; and his 401k is valued at $13,522. At first blush, Joe's net worth appears to be $368,022. Not bad, considering the typical middle-class family has a net worth of about $57,000, right?

However, Joe owes $299,600 on his house; he owes $3,240 and $20,500 on his cars (yes, he's upside-down on the newer one); he has $12,942 in credit card debt; and he had to take a $3,500 loan against his 401k for his daughter's braces. Oh, and don't forget that $10,000 home equity loan he took out to redo the bathroom (a project he's never actually started, yet all the money has somehow disappeared).

Totaling up Joe's debts tells us he owes $349,782. So Joe's real net worth is more like $18,240. That's not even enough for one year of top-name college tuition. Turns out, Joe is 55 years old. He's supposed to retire in 10 years. What's he going to live on?

For the record, Joe is an executive director and makes a pretty decent salary. He brings home about $380,000 annually, plus bonuses. So why isn't Joe better off? Because, like most people, he has confused net worth (wealth) with wages. In his struggle to get that high-paying job, he's spent a lot of time and money and effort trying to "look the part."

There is an old adage that says, "You can never make more than you can spend." That may not be entirely true for someone extremely wealthy—like Bill Gates—because they would be required to spend millions of dollars every day. However, for the rest of us, more normal people, it's very true. Search the Internet for "celebrity bankruptcies" and you'll see what I mean.

You can't become wealthy by making $10 million a year while spending $11 million—even if the banks let you do it. A wage is just a wage and has surprisingly little to do with your eventual net worth.

What factors in to actual wealth is your level of self-control and how much of your wage you're able to hold back and put aside. Recall from the video that the bottom 50 percent of the country owns about half a percent of the stocks and bonds. That means that they aren't investing. Figures on consumer debt and savings rates tell us that they aren't saving either.

In other words, however much money they may—or may not—be making, they're spending it all. They aren't growing their net worth. For most people, their only real investment is their house (assuming they are in a position to even buy one and keep it). That means that most people are tying up nearly all their investment dollars in real estate—whether they know it or not.

So think back to Joe. His net worth is under $20,000 and he's only 10 years from "retirement age." Contrast him with another fictitious example named John. John just bought his first home. Between the first and second mortgages, he owes about $239,000 on his $240,000 home. He has $10,000 in the bank, $7,000 in an IRA, and cars worth $2,500 and $6,000. He also has a student loan for about $5,000—but no credit card debt. Amazingly, John has a net worth of $21,500.

But let's look a little closer here. Joe's cars are newer and worth more. Joe's house is larger and nicer. Joe may have a little less in the bank, yet he's got almost double in his retirement account. The reason John has a higher net worth and is, therefore, wealthier than Joe is because John has restrained himself and stayed satisfied rather than spending everything he makes to keep up appearances.

Of all the people I have helped become millionaires, only a very few are able to exercise this kind of discipline. Most want to start buying the bigger, fancier homes, the bigger, fancier cars and the fancier (sometimes bigger) clothes. Those things just reduce net worth, rather than increase it. So, instead of building their wealth, these people are actually reducing their net worth just to put on a good show. Ironically, they are reducing their chances of ever entering the top one percent in their efforts to look more like they already belong.

THE TOP ONE PERCENT TODAY

As it turns out, just to slip into the bottom end of the top one percent in America, you need to have a net worth of at least $13 million. I'll tell you right now that my intentions don't go quite that far. I want to help people become millionaires. I'm less concerned about getting people into the top one percent.

No one needs that much money to be set up well enough to find financial security and financial freedom. That said, if you'll read, study, understand, and apply my lessons, you can be a millionaire. Whether you reach the top one percent after that or not is up to you. I'll give you the tools and the paradigm you need to get started; how far you take it is your own decision.

So think about what net worth means and whether or not you're ready to make some changes to start growing your net worth. When you are, continue to Lesson 2. Until then, consider watching the video again. Think about what it would mean to you to have real wealth.

Why is it that you want wealth? Is it so you can "afford" to buy nice things and look successful? I can tell you now that you're thinking along the wrong lines. If that's your motivation, you need to stop and reconsider. That kind of motivation is what brought down so many of my friends after I helped build them up.

The first thing for you to do is put away that shopping list. We're not going on this journey together to help you get all that "stuff" on your list. We're going on this journey together so you can start to see that what you have on that list isn't nearly as important as you think it is and that you have deeper priorities you need to fulfill before you start worrying about toys and trinkets.

If you want to be wealthy and successful, you have to change your mindset. You must develop the characteristics that wealthy, successful people have. As Dolly Levi says in the play, "The Matchmaker:" "Money, pardon the expression, is like manure; it isn't worth a thing unless it's spread around, encouraging young things to grow." Keep that in mind as we go forward.

CHARACTERISTICS
OF THE WEALTHY

Any number of stereotypes abound when we think about the wealthiest one percent of Americans. These stereotypes range from sayings about silver spoons and inheritance, to popular opinions about paying a fair share and tax evasion, to blanket generalities about political affiliation. Really, it's quite surprising what people will dream up to label the super-wealthy.

First of all, about 47 percent of the wealthy are Democrats; about 52 percent are Republican. The margin of error in between is for the Independents. So, while the wealthy may sit on both sides of the fence, neither side has the advantage in terms of money. This is good because it means neither side can truly buy an election.

Second, as the video said, the bottom 90 percent of Americans do not own stocks—about half a percent of the total value of stocks is spread between all of them. The upper one percent, on the other hand, derive almost all their net worth from stocks. They call it equity at that level, and it represents ownership in a business.

When you own part of a business, your net worth grows right along with the business—and you don't even have to do anything. If you own 10 percent of XYZ Corp and it releases a new product that increases the stock value from $100 to $110, your own stock holding increases in value from $10 to $11. And, if XYZ Corp is publicly traded, you don't even have to live in a state where XYZ does business—much less work there—to derive that benefit.

As far as inheritances go, in the bottom 90 percent of households, 1 in 5 inherited money. In the top one percent, however, only 1 in 25 inherited money. The rest earned it—usually through careful investment with high returns and some good old-fashioned hard work. The spoons may be made of silver and they may be bigger among the top one percent, but the rest of the country is more likely to get something from the wealthy. If you want to see how this works, look at Bill Gates' plan for his money when he passes. Very little of it will go to his children; the rest will go to various foundations.

When it comes to money management, the bottom 90 percent average around $6,200 in credit card debt and make payments on that debt from month to month. The upper one percent, surprisingly, have no credit card debt. Of course they use credit cards, totaling up bills almost double that of the bottom 90 percent. But the big difference is that they pay that bill in full every month rather than carrying a balance and paying interest.

In terms of credit, the average credit score among the bottom 90 percent is around 640. For the upper one percent, that average number is closer to 705. This means that they don't have perfect credit on average (an 850 score), but they do tend to have better credit, which implies a better ability to manage their credit—including a better record of paying on time. If you want to make it really difficult to build wealth, saddle yourself with a bunch of debt and then start making late payments.

Now let's put the idea of "fair share" and taxes into perspective. Let's suppose the average wage-earner makes $20 a week. Obviously, real people make much more than that, but it's easier to understand what's really happening when we deal in smaller, more comprehensible numbers. Most of us can't wrap our heads around a million dollars, let alone a billion or more. So the average wage earner makes about $20 a week. We'll say that same person pays $5 of that $20 in taxes. For some of you, the idea of paying 25 percent in taxes is appalling. Others would welcome such a low rate.

In this scenario, one of our super-wealthy friends might be making $1,000 dollars a week (only 50 times more—remember, the video said that CEOs sometimes make 380 times more) and this person pays only 20 percent in taxes. How is that fair? The average person pays more in taxes than the super wealthy and they're the ones who can't afford it, right?

Hang on. Let's do the math.

The average person pays only $5 a week; the super-wealthy person pays $200 per week. So who is really paying more in taxes? The fact of the matter is that the government is built on a model that derives most of its income from the super wealthy. The state of California, for instance, gets as much as 60 percent of its annual tax revenue from the wealthiest one percent of its population. If you were to ask someone in the bottom 90 percent to go out and raise as much money as they could right now, on average, they would pull in all their available credit and return with maybe $3,800. In the top one percent, about 57,000 of them could cash out for $30 million.

The point in all this isn't to impress you with the financial holdings of the top one percent. The idea is to help you see some of the patterns and trends that the top one percent share of which the bottom 90 percent don't take part. I also want to dispel a couple of the myths around that top one percent, myths often reinforced and perpetuated by the media.

DIFFERENCES

Now that we've looked at some of those statistics, I want to double-down on the differences between the bottom 90 percent and the top one percent. As I do this, let me point out that the top one percent are not necessarily any better in terms of character. I don't want anyone to feel less of a person just because their net worth isn't measured in the millions. However, if you're reading this book, there's a good chance you want your own net worth to increase. If you really want to make that happen, then you should start taking some lessons from people who have already made it happen.

The problem is that too many people think being wealthy (especially being super wealthy) is all about eating at fancy restaurants, attending headliner events, throwing the pitch for the first baseball game of the season, wearing expensive clothing, and driving exotic sportscars. That's not what being wealthy is all about.

Most of the people you know—those who are already wealthy—don't do most of those things, or at least they don't do them very often. People who have the wealthy mindset are driven by an instinctual need to make their money grow—to increase their net worth and build more wealth. They may or may not even realize it when it happens, but that drive moves them all the same.

People who aren't wealthy—especially those who were wealthy but aren't anymore—don't have that drive. Instead, they share a drive to exploit their money – to use it to make them look better. There's no harm in looking nice or going out to a fancy restaurant—so long as you can afford it—but you need to make sure you keep your pride in check or it will spend all your wealth and leave you wanting.

To highlight more of the difference between the wealthy and the average wage-earner, I'm going to give single sentences followed by short, clarifying paragraphs. Keep in mind that some people with lots of money are still "poor," and some people with very little current wealth are actually already "rich" in terms of these attributes. If you develop all the attributes of the "rich" in these examples, you'll eventually become wealthy—it will only be a matter of time. So, as you read these differences, pay special attention to those where you find yourself described within the "poor" group. What needs to change to get you over onto the "rich" side of the equation? Keep a list of those needed changes as you go.

The rich believe they *create* their lives, but the poor believe that life *happens* to them.

Bad things happen to everyone. How we deal with them is our own choice. "I was born this way" or "the system is rigged against me" are common phrases among the truly poor. They tend to want to go outside themselves and look for somewhere (or someone) to place the blame. This desire to place blame stems from a lack of will (laziness) to change their circumstances. They would rather complain about their fate than work to correct it.

The rich, on the other hand, take responsibility for what's going on and work to change it for the better. The rich will be handed lemons and choose to make lemonade.

The rich play to *win* and the poor play to *lose*.

Believe it or not, the rich are rich because they want to be. The poor are poor because they want to be. That doesn't mean that the poor enjoy being poor; it just means that the poor are unwilling to do what's necessary to be rich, so they choose to stay poor instead. They aren't bad people, necessarily; they just don't have a rich mindset.

The rich are committed to being rich and the poor just "want" to be rich.

Again, the rich will do what it takes to reach their goals. The poor just "want" to be rich—they want someone else to give them the riches so that they don't have to work for them. Where the rich are willing to put in the time and effort—slogging through trenches beneath their self-perceived pay grade—the poor just see hardship and persecution.

The rich think *big* and the poor think *small*.

The poor tend to focus only on what they already know. They are often hesitant to look for the "bigger picture." The rich, on the other hand, tend to look at the "big picture" first and then they figure out ways to make their current situation fit that bigger picture. This vision enables them to keep moving forward in situations where someone poor would shut down from an apparent dead end—tunnel vision.

The rich focus on opportunity and the poor on obstacles.

The rich recognize that life isn't easy. They take on difficulties and work through to earn the rewards on the other side. Many of them relish the challenge and the chance to prove themselves. Over time, they grow almost desensitized to the difficulties—taking every new "curve ball" as a normal part of business. The poor tend to get hung up on the difficulties and what would be required to make it through. Because they are unwilling to look past the problems and focus on the opportunities, they get discouraged easily and tend to quit when the going gets tough. Additionally, this focus on challenges means that all they see are challenges—bigger and bigger ones all the time.

The rich *admire* other rich and successful people and the poor *resent* rich and successful people.

They won't admit it, but deep down most poor people are envious of the rich, surprisingly not for their wealth but for their drive and willpower. This makes poor people resent rich people (after all, poor people could cultivate their own inner drive and become wealthy, too) because they are a constant reminder of inner failure. This is why a favorite past-time for poor people is to speculate on what laws a person had to break to get rich—the poor are trying to help themselves feel better about their own lack of will and direction.

Rich people, on the other hand, seek out the company of other driven, successful people—they want to swap tips and ideas. The rich are so much more comfortable with themselves because they have proof of their accomplishments.

The rich associate with *positive,* successful people and the poor with *negative* people.

As they say, "birds of a feather flock together." Poor people tend to seek out enablers—people who say, "it's okay to be mediocre;

it's okay not to try." These people tend to have little in the way of accomplishment, so the poor end up sitting around and consoling one another, pretending they haven't brought their failures upon themselves. The poor look for people to commiserate with. By the way, the root of "commiserate" is misery.

The rich, on the other hand, look for people who are ready to tackle new challenges. They want people with a "never say die" attitude. People like that tend to be optimistic and positive. Interestingly, positive people are more charismatic; charismatic people tend to be more successful.

The rich are willing to promote themselves and their values while the poor keep quiet about theirs.

The rich tend to feel passionately about things—that's why they're able to take an idea and push it through to completion. That passion bubbles over into a desire to share with others. The rich end up talking about accomplishments and the values needed to reach their goals. The poor have very little in the way of accomplishment; so, no matter how strongly they may feel, they tend to discount themselves and their opinions and stay quiet.

The rich are *bigger* than their problems and the poor are *smaller* than theirs.

This goes back to where a person places his or her focus. When people focus on opportunities and solutions, they tend to work their way over, around, or through their problems. When people focus on the problems, however, they tend to run right into them. Think about driving your car down the freeway. Can you stay in your lane if you're always staring into oncoming traffic? We tend to go where we focus. The rich think bigger than their problems and go toward success; the poor think smaller than their problems and run right into them.

The rich choose to get paid based on results and the poor choose to get paid based on their time.

You will never get rich working for an hourly wage. It's not that the wages themselves are too small; it's that working for an hourly wage enforces a different mindset in a person. If you are punching a clock, you have no incentive to work hard or dream up new, more efficient ways to accomplish a task. After all, if you're getting paid to fill a seat, you'll just end up with new work to replace the old work that you just completed. It's not that a person can't build wealth on an hourly wage, it's just their mindset that holds them back. Rich people want to be paid for their results because they have confidence that they can create new methods and save time, thereby making the same money in less time. That's why rich people seek out bonuses and commission structures and poor people seek out big salaries.

The rich think "both" and the poor think "either/or."

Rich people are always looking for solutions, especially win-win solutions. They want to have their cake and eat it too. They want to think up new ways to make exciting things happen. Poor people tend to think in terms of limits and established norms. They think in terms of what has been done before. They think in terms of exclusion. Poor people want to divide the pie in such a way that they get the biggest possible piece. Rich people go out and bake a bigger pie and then share that pie with as many people as possible.

The rich focus on their net worth and the poor focus on their working income.

We've talked about this one pretty extensively already. The poor want to see that their work is being valued now, and they want the highest reward possible for the work they are doing this instant. They also want to display their success at the earliest possible moment.

The rich are less concerned with their wages because they know they can earn two dollars and then grow that two into four. Because they have confidence in their ability to grow their money, the wage itself becomes less important. Instead, having enough wealth to take advantage of opportunities becomes important.

The rich manage their money and the poor are managed by theirs.

The poor, regardless of their wage, often find that they have more month left at the end of the money instead of more money at the end of the month. They "want" so many things that they tend to spend money the moment it comes in. The rich, on the other hand, make sure to monitor their inflows and outflows. The rich, regardless of their wage, make sure they spend less than they make so they can have some left over in the future.

The rich have their money work hard for them while the poor work hard for their money.

No one is disputing that the poor work hard (the ones that work, anyway). In fact, many of them work even harder than the rich. This is because they are working hard for that new car or new TV or new pair of shoes. They see something they want and then they work hard for it. The rich look at money in a totally different way. Instead of working for that TV or car or whatever, the rich work hard for a new investment vehicle and then let IT work hard for the TV or car or whatever. Then, when the investment has finished working on the TV or car, it can go to work on something else—without the rich person needing to earn the money themselves.

The rich act in spite of fear and the poor let fear control them.

The rich are willing to take risks because they know they can't ever lose their most valuable asset—themselves. The poor are scared to take risks because they've spent too much time and effort fixating over their money; the chance that it might be lost is a chance they won't take. It's not that the rich don't see the dangers in investing; the rich also see the potential and justify the risk in favor of the return. The poor can't get past the idea that they might lose their money—since they tend to spend most or all of it and have very little left over in the first place.

The rich constantly learn and grow and the poor think they already know it all.

The rich recognize that there is far more knowledge in the world than one person could ever know in a single lifetime. They keep an open mind, searching for new opportunities. The rich will educate themselves on new possibilities and chances in order to make better decisions.

The poor tend to close themselves off. They want to "do it alone" so that they don't have to give credit to anyone else. This attitude tends to mean that they refuse outside assistance and ideas, locking themselves into a particular pattern and never leaving it. While the determination is commendable, the stubborn resistance to positive change makes it extremely difficult for poor people to develop new skills and "get ahead" in the world.

GAINING COMMITMENT

When I moved from Wyoming back to Price during my employment as a government worker, I thought I knew all there was to know. I thought I was on track. I thought I was doing well. Joining up with the Jaycees, however, showed me how out of bounds I was. It opened my eyes to new possibilities and helped me understand that the little I did know was just the tip of the iceberg.

Joining the Jaycees was one of those pivotal moments that molded me into a rich person, long before I had any wealth of which to speak. I'm not sure I'd have had the courage to try a new, different opportunity had I not been strong-armed into that first Jaycees meeting.

After that, however, there was no stopping me. I took to that leadership culture like a fish to water. I drank in everything they had to offer, and by the time they kicked me out at age 35 I was ready to be so much more than the government worker I'd been to that point. I didn't want to work for time anymore; I wanted a chance to work for real results and be able to demonstrate those results.

I don't know if there's an organization like the Jaycees in your area, but you might look into it. It's never too late to start developing the mindset and characteristics of a rich person; it's never too early either. I believe on the old proverb: "The best time to plant a tree was 20 years ago; the next best time is now."

Perhaps more importantly, no matter how much you earn, you'll never really start amassing wealth until you start to think like a person who understands wealth. You might get yourself into a higher-paying job, but human nature will push you to spend that raise, not turn it into real wealth. It's time to wrap your head around that and start thinking like a rich person. Start looking for opportunities to do and be more than you currently are—especially opportunities that reward you for your efforts and results, not just your time.

In the next chapter, I will cover what you need to do, specifically, to begin building your net worth. I can promise you, however, that you'll find the steps to be almost impossible if you don't develop the mindset first, so don't rush ahead. Feel free to spend a little time here meditating about these concepts. Move on when you're ready—when you're truly committed

BE HONEST WITH YOURSELF: CAN YOU DO THIS?

TIME FOR A MOMENT OF INTROSPECTIVE truth: do you really think you can be wealthy? Do you really think there is any hope that, one day, you could be rich? If not, thanks for reading up to this point in the book, but you might as well stop here.

If you don't think you can be better—do better—then you won't. That drive has to come from within. I can give you the tools to get there (and I will, starting in this chapter) but you have to be willing to follow the steps. You have to have the discipline to stick with it—no matter how tough it gets.

Most people will say they're ready but they really aren't. I dare say that 99.9 percent of people won't ever really give my formula a shot because they perceive it as too hard or too much. They want an easier road. They don't want to put in the hard work, time, and effort required to reach true wealth.

That's fine.

There's nothing wrong with not being wealthy. Most people (at least 90 percent, right?) pass through life without hitting that mark. Most people don't even really want to be wealthy. Most of them just want a good, stable, 9 to 5 job with a good salary so they can pay all their bills and have a little extra for vacations or fun. It's not a bad thing to want that kind of life, but if you do want to become wealthy, that kind of life—without taking some extra steps—will not get you to wealth. That kind of mindset does not focus on building net worth.

I would say probably 80 percent of Americans really only want that kind of life. And I would guess that most of these people—though not quite all—are content with their lives…happy, even. So you don't need to feel like a failure if you back out now. You can still be happy without being wealthy. Then again, maybe you just need to spend more time in the first two lessons to better develop your mindset, or maybe you'll never wrap your head around it.

The choice, ultimately, is yours.

That said, if you continue on from here, I will be expecting you to follow the formula and become wealthy. If you decide to find your own path before reading on, that's fine. Once you start reading beyond this point, however, you are committing to yourself and to me that you will stick this through to the end.

DO SOMETHING DIFFERENT

As we have already discussed, you need to begin changing your mindset. After all, you're not going to be successful thinking the way you have up to this point, or you would already be successful, and you wouldn't be reading these lessons.

It rains on the rich and the poor in approximately the same amounts and for the same periods of time. There is no roulette wheel for life to dictate that one person should get rich while the next-door neighbor stays poor. Many people believe in luck, but I've found that, as I've said, the harder you work, the luckier you get. This concept applies in two ways: if you change your mind set about wealth you will change your mind set about the way you look at problems and opportunities.

We've already talked extensively in the first two lessons about changing your mindset regarding wealth. It's not about how much you earn; it's about what you do with that money that counts—it's about spending and minding the back door. Think through items and events in terms of their impact on your net worth and then decide accordingly. You don't always need to choose the option that directly increases or maintains your net worth, but you need to be increasing and maintaining more often than you are decreasing, or you will have no net worth to speak of.

The other way you need to change your mindset is about problems and opportunities. Everyone gets hit by problems. When I was running Phone Directories Company, we had ups and downs all the time. At one point, I owed my printer about $3 million. That's a significant chunk of change for any business. Most people would consider this a serious problem, and they would be right.

In my case, however, we had the money – it was just tied up in the business. To pull it out and pay the printer would have meant putting on the brakes for growth. It was a problem, but it was also an opportunity. By working closely with him, he in effect was loaning me the $3 million so I could grow the business enough to repay him. I was able to make sure that we got him enough money to cover his needs when those needs arose without needing to close out the debt right away.

Am I happy that I owed my printer so much money? I certainly would have preferred to have had the free cash to pay him. He's a good man, and a great business partner, and I lost a lot of sleep because I couldn't pay him sooner. That said, his patience proved to be a huge opportunity for us to continue growing the business until we could afford to pay him—in full.

We were able to do this in one year and it ultimately made the two of us close business partners. He could have probably taken me to court and tried to exact the money from me immediately, but it would have been expensive for both of us and he wouldn't have received full payment as attorneys always get more than their share. Instead, we were able to work together to turn what could have been a big problem into a great opportunity for collaboration and success for both parties. It took faith and a lot of communication on both sides, but we did it.

PAY YOURSELF BEFORE YOU PAY YOUR BILLS

Okay, hopefully you're starting to think like a wealthy person, looking at money and problems differently than you once did. Now it's time to take action. The first way you can begin to turn any amount of income, whether it be a modest wage or a fairly robust salary, into wealth is to pay yourself before you pay your bills. This is one of the keys to creating wealth on any income.

When you earn money, the first thing you must do is pay taxes. How much depends on your tax bracket, but Uncle Sam wants his share and he'll get it or throw you in jail. The next thing I do is pay 10% of my earnings to my church. In my mind, it's my way of giving back to God and thanking him for blessing me with the energy, ingenuity, knowledge, and "luck" to have any success in the first place. Maybe you don't have a similar belief, but my point is that you need to learn to be charitable: give back, pay it forward. I highly recommend that you cultivate charity and find some place to give back. My rule for building wealth follows right in this vein.

The next thing you do with your money, and this is the most important thing to learn, is to pay yourself. You've already given 10 percent to the Lord or to your charity; now it's time to pay yourself. You need to take 10 percent of your earnings and set them aside for future growth.

When I was growing my business, I was putting every spare penny back into the business—often more than 10 percent. I recommend 10 percent because it's an easier target, but you need to look at that 10 percent as a minimum. If you can discipline yourself to put in more than 10 percent, you will accelerate yourself on the path to wealth. Still, for starters, 10 percent is a good goal and you can always increase your contribution later.

After you've set aside that 10 percent, you can pay your bills and go on vacation with whatever's left over. If you can't pay your bills on that amount, you need to watch the back door and cut your expenses until you can pay your bills and set aside that 10 percent.

There is no other viable way to get yourself up out of the 90 percent into the top 10 percent of wealth. Playing the lottery is the only option for leapfrogging from the bottom 90 percent to the top 10 percent without working your way through all the intermediate steps. However, you have a much better chance of walking out your door, right now, and getting struck by lightning—even if it's a clear day outside than you do of winning the lottery. The lottery is probably the worst investment you could possibly make because your chance of return is essentially zero. Besides, people who don't earn their way into wealth tend to waste the money, burn up all the net worth, and end up right back where they started—or worse. They are too busy singing "If I Were a Rich Man" along with Tevye to watch the back door.

As simple as it is, this rule of saving 10 percent is surprisingly difficult for many people. The reason is that you are the only one who can punish yourself for failure. And, worse than that, unless you are the one to invent the time machine (in which case, you can just go back in time and invest in a little startup called Microsoft or Apple or McDonald's or... you get the picture), you're only going to be able to punish yourself in the future, which is not now and, therefore, carries very little weight for most people in the here and now.

The other difficulty for people is leaving the money alone. Once they set it aside, they want to touch it again. When I talk about this concept with people in person, I tell them that there are only two times when they can ever draw from this money, and both times will directly increase or preserve their net worth. I'll give you the same two situations.

The first is to buy a home. You can dip into this money to purchase a home because, over the long run, the value of that home will increase and so will your net worth. Additionally, I believe that renting is just throwing away money to someone else. You may have times in life when you need to rent, but I think that everyone should own their own home. This doesn't mean that everyone will own a big, fancy mansion. On the contrary, many people should only buy a smaller house— especially if the kids are gone. How many rooms do you really need, after all? More rooms just means more work to maintain and more property taxes and more utility costs. Don't buy more house than you need.

The second situation when it is okay to dip into savings is when your life is on the line. If you get sick and need to use some of this savings to pay a doctor to help you get better, that's okay. You're not worth anything to anyone if you're dead (other than maybe a life insurance policy payout), so it's better to use some of this money so you can start contributing.

It will take discipline to set aside this money and not touch it. At first, you will be strongly tempted to use it every time it grows big enough for you to afford something you want.

Don't do it! Don't touch it!

If the temptation is too strong, you might consider getting an account that requires two signatures to access the money, that way you can't go and raid it during a drunken fit or moment of weakness. Over time, it will become more of a habit, and you won't think about it so much.

Again, you've still got 80 percent of your after-tax income to do with whatever you choose. You can't go to the government during the year and say, "Excuse me, I changed my mind and I'd like those tax dollars back." You need to treat this 10 percent the same way. It's untouchable. Learn how to survive on the rest of your income. Discipline yourself, and leave this money alone. Without it, you'll never be wealthy.

THE TWO BIGGEST WEALTH KILLERS

Once you've decided to start paying yourself that 10 percent and you've started to shift your mindset to match the rich, you are likely to face two big problems. The first is procrastination; the second is instant gratification.

Procrastination is the number one killer of the 90 percent. Anyone can recognize a good idea when they see it; people aren't generally dumb. So why, if people can recognize good ideas, don't more people act on those ideas? Well, think about your last New Year's Resolution. The last time you made a New Year's Resolution, what happened? Did you stick with it? Did you even start it? What was the process you used to come up with that resolution? Many people will come to the end of the year and realize something that they want to change about themselves. This could be as early as September or October, depending on the person. Do they immediately start working on that change? Of course not. New Year's Eve is coming, and it would be better to start out the New Year with a bang, right?

The problem is, the moment you start thinking that way you are putting off the change and, whether you realize it or not, you will start to talk yourself out of it. After all, no matter how important it may have seemed, every day you go without that change is another day you've survived, so why make the change if you don't need to go through the effort in order to continue surviving?

And that's why people fail.

By the time the New Year rolls around, they have already talked themselves out of their original commitment but they just don't realize it yet. So don't put off important things. If it's important enough for you to do it, it's important enough for you to start now. If it's not important enough that you need to start now, don't plan on thinking it's important enough to start later. That's the nature of procrastination.

The second killer, perhaps even bigger than the first one, is instant gratification. Most people have just enough discipline to get started. They start saving or start changing their mindset and then they look at the dollar signs in their savings account. When they see the money accumulating there, however, they don't see the money's long-term potential in terms of wealth and growth opportunities. Instead, they see a down payment on that new car, a new wardrobe, or a set of new appliances. They have thoughts like, "I deserve it. My neighbor has one (or two), so I should, too. It's not fair that he (or she) has all these toys and I don't. I've got the credit—the bank believes I can afford it, so why not? I'll buy it today and pay it off in the future. I'll be more respected once I have the thing, and it'll make me feel good."

They think that because they have the money available to spend that they can actually "afford" to spend it. Nothing could be further from the truth. Availability is not the same as affordability. If you choose to spend one dollar today, you will not have that dollar tomorrow. You need to ask yourself every time you are tempted to spend if you can actually afford to lose that dollar because once it's gone, it's gone forever. While it's true that it can be re-earned again, the time needed to maximize that dollar and earn more money is lost forever.

The reality of the situation is that much of what we want to buy forces us to go into debt to get it. But debt is the opposite of net worth. No matter what you might think you deserve, loading up on debt to acquire a bunch of toys in order to "keep up with the Joneses" will only sink you. It's that line of thinking that led to the U.S. financial collapse of 2007 and 2008. It's that line of thinking that has the net worth of the median household falling, instead of growing. We keep "inventing" new toys, gadgets, and gizmos. You will never be able to afford them all, so stop trying.

If you can't develop the discipline to budget like we've talked about—living on 80 percent of your after-tax income—you will never make it into the top 10 percent.

Period.

As an aside, living on that after-tax 80 percent means not using any more credit than you can pay off in a month. You might use your credit cards to buy things during the month, but it's absolutely the worst way to purchase if you're not going to pay off the bill in full because of the high interest rates. Compare that to a home loan (often 5 percent or less) or an auto loan (frequently 7 percent or less). Credit cards are three times as expensive as most other forms of credit. Still, they are a useful tool for consolidation, convenience, and protection—and the rewards points can be a nice bonus. The catch is that you must not carry a balance.

If you're having trouble living on your 80 percent after-tax income, consider cutting up your credit and debit cards and living on a cash-only basis for a while. You'd be amazed at how easy it is to spend money when you don't see the actual cash, and how much easier it is to say no to a great sale when you have to hand over your hard-earned, hard currency to pay for the merchandise. It's a lot easier to watch the back door this way.

When it comes down to it, people don't typically run into trouble on the big purchases alone. They run into trouble because they make some big purchases and then make a lot of little purchases. The little purchases seem easier to pay for, so they get paid first (plus a little money pays a lot of small bills, so the payer feels better inside). Pretty soon, however, there isn't enough money for the big items like cars and houses. It's amazing how many people still go shopping for new "stuff"— on credit, no less—even while they're facing foreclosure.

You can go without that new set of tools or that new blouse. You can go without dinner at that fancy new restaurant across town. You can drive the same car for 15 years or more. If you want to look like the 90 percent—with all the new stuff all the time—then you will likely live a life of instant gratification just like the 90 percent and one day realize you have absolutely nothing to show for it.

I hope you are realizing this one point: Instant gratification and net worth don't get along very well. Instant gratification is why celebrities can make millions per year and still end up totally broke. What's more, instant gratification in financial matters tends to bleed over into instant gratification in other areas of life.

This is a chapter on wealth, not relationships, but if you can't be disciplined enough to handle your money, your lack of self-discipline will probably cost you in other areas of life also. I've seen it time and again.

KNOW WHERE THE DOUGH GOES

One of the critical things you must know, when on the quest for wealth, is where your money is going. We talked about the dangers of instant gratification and how you can send more out the back door in a teaspoon than you can bring in through the front with a scoop shovel. One of the problems that many people have is that they don't watch the back door—they do not track their spending so they have no idea where all the money goes. They are certain they make enough to pay all their bills and then some, but they always end up with more *month* at the end of the *money*.

How does this happen?

It happens because most people don't have adequate controls. They see something they want, they know they make enough money to pay all the bills and have a little to spare, and they buy what they want. They justify that "one time won't hurt." What does that sound like? In some ways, spending money is like using drugs. You don't realize how all the little instances are going to add up until you've lost yourself in the thrill and can't quit. The easiest thing is to just not get started in the first place.

One way to help you see where your money goes is to keep all your receipts. Get a piece of graph paper (or use a computer) and keep a running column of everything you spend—every single penny. If you buy a new car, put it on the list. If you buy a gum ball for your kid, put it on the list. Recurring payments for things like health insurance, mortgage, and utilities go on there, too. Figure the monthly cost of home owners and/or auto insurance and put them on the list as well.

In one column, name the expense: groceries, mortgage, new shirt, gum ball for Timmy, etc. In the next column, record how much you spent. In the third column, justify that purchase. Then, at the end of every week—week, not month—sit down and total everything up. Surprised at how much you spent? Keep this list, and you will quickly find that you start to spend less. Most people don't even realize the money is sneaking out the back door and that's because they're spending it on trivial items that seem small, even insignificant, at the time.

Everyone needs food, clothing, and shelter to survive, but we often buy food we don't need, clothes that won't last, and too much shelter. Remember that you are trying to build your net worth. Don't throw it away on excess. This doesn't mean you need to live on starvation diets. You can buy good food to stock your home but you need to watch out for the number of times you eat out—even if it's just a quick stop for ice cream or a hot dog. Even the dollar menu adds up. Stop eating out just because it's more convenient. The time you waste waiting for a table and the money you waste paying the inflated margins is gone forever. Save that for special occasions and eat at home or pack a lunch the rest of the time.

Clothes are a sign of the times. If you don't have the right clothes nowadays, you'll be ignored or looked down on. Well, we'll see who's looking down when you are part of the 10 percent club and they are still trying to buy the latest, "greatest" fashion on maxed out credit cards. Clothes should be functional, and they should last. And you can be stylish on a budget. Consider shopping thrift stores and garage sales. You can often find all the designer labels at pennies on the dollar.

Finally, be careful with the amount of money you spend on a home. I almost hesitate to tell you what kind of home to buy, but I'll offer some advice. Really think about what you need. Does the dog need its own bedroom? Can't your kids share a room? How are you going to maintain that place when you are old? What are the property taxes going to look like? What about utilities? Frequently, lottery winners will go out and buy a huge house to showcase their winnings. Unfortunately, big houses come with big yearly tax bills, not to mention the maintenance costs for cleaning and landscaping.

Buy a modest house and pay it off. If you really want something bigger, you can sell your existing home (or rent it) to help pay for the next one. This is how it used to be done. Nowadays, kids come out of college and want to buy the huge, six-bedroom, four-bathroom house up on the hill because that's what their parents owned. The kids don't realize that their parents probably worked 20 years before buying into that big house. You need to do the same.

Start small and work your way up. And never take on a home equity loan to buy yourself toys. A house will be the biggest source of net worth for most people. Don't risk your most valuable asset just for some new toys. The only time you should be dipping into your equity is when you're betting the farm on a twice-in-a-lifetime opportunity. Even then, I would recommend not involving the house, if it's your primary residence. There's always a chance the venture will fail, and then you'll be broke and homeless. It's better to avoid risking the homestead, if at all possible.

HOW TO START

Today, write down a list of the things you can do to get started. Set yourself some benchmarks about what you want to do financially and when you want to complete them. Be realistic. I made it to $5 million in five years, just like I told the Price Chamber of Commerce that I would; however, I had an opportunity right in front of me and I was willing to work to make it happen. Be honest with yourself about the opportunities you have available and start small.

Also, figure out where you ultimately want to be financially. What is your end goal? How will you know when you've "made it"? Write all these things down. You could put them in a journal or in a special file on the computer; I don't really care where you write them so long as they are written. Record your current net worth in that same place. You need to be able to look back on where you started and look forward at where you want to go and you can't do that if you never write down your goals.

Chances are, you'll make some mistakes along the way but don't let them keep you down. We all make mistakes, but giving up is not an option, even if you fail one, 10, or even 100 times. We can't give up because of one, 10, or even 100 mistakes. You just have to get back up, brush yourself off and start going again.

Now that you've got your list, refer to it often. Go back and look at the things you said you were going to do. Make them happen. Don't chicken out just because it's hard. Prove that you've got what it takes. Remember, you committed to do this when you started reading this section.

BECOMING A MILLIONAIRE

THIS IS YOUR FINAL CHANCE. In order for your trajectory in life to change, you have to change. It's that simple. If you want things to get better, then you have to get better. You need to start setting aside your 10 percent right now, if you haven't started already. The rest of the lessons will be worthless to you if you can't act on them, and the only way to act on them is to be setting aside money so you are in a position to put it to work for you.

When I was starting Phone Directories Company, there was no one around to tell me to keep sticking all my money back in the business. In fact, I experienced just the opposite with those who worked with me.

My first partners were trying to take money out as soon as they could. They wanted to sell the golden eggs rather than hatching more golden geese. Even my first wife did quite a bit of dipping into the business. I was surrounded by people who saw a good thing going and wanted a piece of the action. You'll be in the same situation with this 10-percent money.

Your spouse, children, and relatives will all see the money building up and probably all want a piece of the action. Don't let that happen— especially if you are the one trying to cash in on the most action! You must learn to view that money as something other than "money," as strange as that may sound. Look at it, instead, as "net worth" because it is money that is building value for your future, not money that is to be spent. If you don't make enough right now to put away 10 percent then get a better job that pays the bills (or two or three); ask for a raise if it's merited; look back over your receipts and recorded spending and see where you can cut monthly expenses.

It's that simple. It's not easy, but it's that simple.

As you are building your fund for investment, you should start shopping around for a money manager, which is very different from an estate planner. A money manager works to grow your money. An estate planner helps you plan for your eventual passing and organizes your money to help your heirs avoid taxes on any inheritance. Both have their merits, and you'll want an estate planner eventually, but for now you want to focus on growing your money so there is an "estate" to plan for. Also, don't settle for the first manager you interview. Instead, do some research on different managers in your area and try to find one that fits you and your goals. If you can, learn whether a manager is compensated based on salary or by commission.

Money managers are compensated one of two ways, each with different pros and cons. Many money managers are on salary. This is an advantage to you because they are more likely to give you advice that benefits you specifically. Since they are compensated based solely on the accounts they open or money they bring in, they are more likely to consider options that would otherwise be less profitable (like indexed funds).

On the other hand, a salaried manager won't work as hard for your money. They get paid whether you make money or not, so they don't have the same incentive to make sure you are earning a great return. Salaried managers sometimes have other constraints on them as well, like the number of certain types of accounts they need to open or the number of clients they need to service. Constraints like these can also impact your relationship with them and the way they handle your money.

Commissioned managers, on the other hand, are hungry. They have to be. They aren't compensated for sitting at the desk. If they aren't out there bringing in money (both in terms of new clients and returns), they aren't eating. They don't get a paycheck until the firm makes money, which means you need to make money. The flip side is that commissioned agents can sometimes be too hungry. They can be swayed by promises of big rewards on the back end and "advise" clients to invest in sub-optimal products because the manager wants the kickback.

There are laws around this kind of behavior, but it still happens in some cases, so buyer beware. Another thing to watch for is that commissioned agents typically won't work with clients of "small" net worth. The managers make their money by handling large portfolios; if your nest egg is only a few thousand dollars many commissioned managers won't be interested. If they are it might actually qualify as a red flag.

In addition to the manager, make sure to investigate fee schedules and account minimums. It's entirely possible that you'll need to settle for a less-than-the-best manager at first because you don't have enough money to start with. Don't worry; as you grow your wealth, you'll reach a point where you can pull your investment from one manager and move it to the money manager you really want. Be patient, and don't get complacent. Also, if you know you're not with the best it might be a good idea to keep a closer eye on your investments. You don't want to lose everything because your manager made the wrong call. Of course, that bit of advice holds true no matter where you choose to invest—or with whom.

THE MILLIONAIRES NEXT DOOR

Now, while you're thinking about money managers and when to get started with one, let me review with you some facts about the millionaires next door.

First of all, you wouldn't believe they were millionaires even, if you could see their balance sheet. They don't "look" like millionaires, and they don't "act" like millionaires. Most people think, for some strange reason, that millionaires wear expensive clothing, watches, and shoes.

In fact, most millionaires don't even drive this year's model vehicle much less the fancy sportscar or luxury sedan off the showroom floor. They usually live in a modest house, thereby avoiding a heavy property-tax obligation each year, in a middle-class neighborhood. They live on the same street with postal workers, firefighters, secretaries, and mechanics. Most millionaires are married and in terms of the primary wage earner, most are men—about age 57 with three children. Only one in five is retired despite their obvious net worth.

About two-thirds of millionaires are self-employed, but that means fully one-third are not self-employed. Interestingly, only two-thirds of those self-employed actually consider themselves to be entrepreneurs. The doctors, lawyers, and accountants that people so often expect to be millionaires make up the other one-third of the non-entrepreneurial self-employed. So two-thirds of them have created some other type of business and become millionaires in the process.

Half of millionaire households include a stay-at-home mom. Of the mothers who do work outside the home, most are school teachers. The average taxable income for these families is only $131,000, though average income is closer to $250,000. Leveraging just those low salary figures, they have an average net worth of $3.7 million! Nearly 6 percent of the millionaires around have more than $10 million. Only one percent of Americans clear the $13 million mark.

Most millionaires do own their own home—about 97 percent—but the average home value is a mere $320,000. So much for the myth about mansions and millionaires. That means there are six millionaires with homes worth $250,000 for every one millionaire with a home worth $1 million. Again, the problem with a large home is that it requires large overhead and upkeep. Higher utility bills and higher property taxes don't increase net worth.

One of the facts that surprises most people is that many millionaires didn't receive any inheritance. In fact, more than half never received even a single dollar. Less than 20 percent of the millionaires out there inherited 10 percent or more of their wealth, meaning that even those who did inherit some money made far more on their own than they were ever given. Less than 10 percent of millionaires believe they will receive any kind of inheritance in the future—unlike many in the 90 percent who are counting on that inheritance to get them out of the hole they've dug for themselves. Most millionaires believe that America has been a great place for them, a land of opportunity.

Their trick to becoming millionaires? Live well below your means. Typically, the wives handle the household finances and are meticulous planners and budgeters. As a result, most of these families have a "go to hell" fund with enough wealth to live without working for 10 years or more.

They usually save 15 percent of their annual income—which is more than the 10 percent I've recommended. About one in five millionaires isn't a college graduate, but they all believe in the value of education and spend heavily on making sure that their children and grandchildren get the chance to be well educated. They also believe in hard work but still leave time for their families, typically spending between 45 and 55 hours a week working.

Millionaires invest 20 percent of their realized income (take-home pay) on average and hold about 20 percent of that in market securities like stocks and bonds, but they rarely sell these ownership interests except to transfer them to a different firm. They don't pull money out of these investment funds. They are often considered tightwads and maintain friendships with their accountants and lawyers. They are excellent at watching the back door while being, on average, not noticeably better at getting money in the front door.

If you asked the average American to define the term "wealthy," you would most likely hear about fast cars, big houses, and lots of toys. You would hear descriptions of Hollywood pop-stars and athletic superstars. What you wouldn't hear about is restraint or discipline. That's why so many people are destined to "get by" without ever amassing real wealth. As we just discussed, it doesn't matter how much you make, it matters how much you restrain yourself. How little can you live on? You can become a millionaire on any livable wage, the only real variable is how long it will take. Those in the lower 90 percent of America's wealth curve fail to understand this concept and are, therefore, doomed to never grow their wealth and rise out of the poverty they seem drawn to.

DETERMINING IF YOU'RE WEALTHY

I have a simple equation for you to use to determine if you are on track to being wealthy. I like this equation because, until you get to the end of the road, you won't have all of your wealth "in the bank." Also, for someone just starting out, or a few years into the process, it can feel like nothing is happening. Building wealth is like a moving freight train. It takes time to get it started, but it'll keep moving faster and faster until it seems unstoppable.

The formula is to multiply your age by your pretax household income from all sources except inheritance. Then divide by 10. This is what your net worth should be.

In determining whether or not you meet that mark, count only what you've earned yourself; don't count any inherited wealth you may have been fortunate enough to receive. Another way to look at this is to multiple your age by the 10 percent of your income that you should be saving. This means two things: when you are just starting out, you will be behind, and, every time you get a raise, you'll be behind again.

It's not particularly hard to make up for getting a year older. If you just stick with the 10 percent plan, you'll account for each year of age you gain. The difficulty comes when you get a raise or when you're just starting out and need to catch up. When you get a raise, continue to contribute your 10 percent. If possible, keep living on your "old" salary and contribute the entire increase to you investments.

For the gentleman in our example, let's say he got a $10,000 raise and now makes $110,000 annually. Now his net worth target goes up to $440,000. If he increases his standard of living by $10,000, he'll use up all of his raise. But what if he keeps living like he was making just the $100,000? That will give him an extra $10,000 with which to increase his net worth. Of course, he'll need to account for any tax increase and allow for charitable contributions on the increase, but he could have as much as $7,000 to $8,000 left with which to work. Why not combine that with the 10 percent he was already contributing? It makes that $40,000 increase in his net worth target seem much more attainable.

For those of you just starting out, it can feel a little overwhelming. You just got out of school and you're starting your first job. How can you be expected to have so much wealth already? You're not expected to, at least not yet. But you need to pull out all the stops and work your way there. One thing to consider is that, once you can afford a house, that house will count toward your net worth. Of course, any mortgage will count against your net worth, but each time you make a payment, your wealth will increase a bit. If you pay extra the principle each month, your wealth will grow just that much faster.

So there are methods to grow your wealth more quickly, even when you're on a limited budget. In the next lesson, we'll talk about other things you can do to increase your net worth, including how to use the 10 percent you're saving. You want to make it grow on its own, not just because of the 10 percent you continue to contribute, so we'll talk about the risks and rewards of some different investment vehicles.

For now, go find a money manager and sit down for a "free consultation." Don't feel obligated to buy any products or sign up for any programs just now. Simply go and try to get a feel for personality and fit. Find someone you feel you can trust. Even if that person isn't the top of the industry, knowing you can trust him or her will go a long way toward smoothing the process of becoming wealthy.

INVESTMENT VEHICLES

W HEN YOU START INVESTING, remember an important lesson that I learned during those up-and-down years of the early 80s: Don't put all your eggs in one basket. Some people will tell you that diversification is really "di-worse-ification." I can see the wisdom in that from a business standpoint. The idea behind diversification is that the economy is like a whole bunch of roller coasters and you want to maximize your time at the top of the hill. When you operate a business (or invest) you pick one of those roller coasters and start riding. Some roller coasters go really high and really low; others stay a bit more level and don't experience those same swings. Additionally, some roller coasters go up while others go down.

Diversification is the process of choosing several different roller coasters to ride all at the same time in hopes that some will be up while others are down. If you were to ride only one roller coaster (or put all your assets into a single investment vehicle), you would be subject to the same ups and downs at the same times, in the same degrees. If you spread your assets, then some of those roller coasters might be up while others are down, thus preserving—or even growing—your wealth when parts of the market are weak.

But in a business, the risk of diversification is that you get too far from what you're good at. If a car company decided to start making buses, for instance, the concept is simple enough that they could make the leap. If that same company wanted to get into boat building, or aircraft design, on the other hand, the differences start to become too broad. And who wants to think about a car company making video games? Or clothes? Or trying to run a fast food chain?

Some industries are so different from one another that for a business it's not worth the time and effort to learn how to branch out into that industry. At Phone Directories Company, we spread into related industries by printing trade reference directories for such industries as mining. We also made posters of some of our more popular phonebook covers (like the controversial 1985 Jackson Hole cover) and sold them. Ventures like those helped to smooth the ups and downs that the phone directory industry faced, making our business more stable.

On the other hand, when I was deep into bartering, I started the Free Trade Exchange. It was part of Phone Directories Company and helped us to win over advertisers who might not have been able (or willing) to advertise with us otherwise. However, it was a business all in itself, and it required a lot of time, attention, and education that didn't directly relate to the core business of printing directories.

Eventually, as great as it was, it got to be too much. The barter side of the business started to detract from the directories side of the business—the real money-making side. At that point, we closed down the Free Trade Exchange. It was diversification that became too broad to be a benefit.

The same principles hold true for individual investing. You want to diversify into what you know in order to protect yourself from the fluctuations of the market. For instance, when the stock market drops because of currency or market concerns, gold, silver, and other precious metals usually see an increase. The idea is that people start to worry about the collapse of the free market, so they want to shift their money into hard assets (things you can touch or hold), which will outlast the market. If Wall Street shuts down, stocks become worthless pieces of paper but gold, for instance, holds its value.

You just need to be careful about how diversified you get because you'll begin to stray outside the bounds of familiarity. Investing in an asset you don't understand is like turbocharging your risk. You might as well go down to Vegas and put some cash on the roulette wheel. If you don't understand what's going on, you're not investing; you're just gambling. This is why a great money manager is essential. He or she can help you maneuver through the ups and downs of the market and keep you apprised of market conditions and trends.

To give you a better understanding of some various investment vehicles and ways to grow your net worth, let's look at some different ideas. Keep in mind that your money manager may have additional options (or subsets of these options) and can give you more detail than what you'll find here. This is just to help prepare you so you can ask better questions for the next time you meet your money manager—because you've already started meeting with him or her after the last lesson, right?

ASSET CATEGORIES

Whenever you invest, you are taking your money and exchanging it for some other type of asset. Before we go into some of the most common types of investments, there are a couple descriptive terms you should understand. Knowing these will help you better understand how to invest and when to do it.

Liquid Assets: Liquid assets get their name from the nature of liquid: it flows easily from one place to another. Liquid assets are easily transferred from one person to another. These assets are usually easy to find, easy to buy, and easy to sell. Liquid assets are sometimes referred to as "like cash," meaning the ease with which you can move in and out of them to either invest money or cash out.

Illiquid Assets: Obviously, illiquid assets are the opposite of liquid assets. Illiquid assets often have good rates of return, but they are harder to move on the market. They might be rare collections for which it's hard to find the different pieces, or they might be things that involve a lot of paperwork. Assets like these are still useful investments, but you need to be cautious about putting too much of your net worth into them because if you ever need that money quickly, you could be stranded. To move an illiquid asset quickly, you typically have to sell at a huge discount, often resulting in a loss.

Hard Assets: Hard assets are items you can examine with your five senses: sight, sound, taste, touch, and smell. Real estate is an example of a hard asset. Precious metals can be a hard asset if you hold the actual metals in your possession. Some investment firms will hold the metal for you and send you a certificate stating the value. Art and other collectibles are also hard assets. The advantage of a hard asset is that it's in your possession so you don't have to worry about trying to round it up or track it down if you decide to cash out. The disadvantage is that someone can break into your house and take it. Additionally, hard assets tend to be more illiquid. You can move gold and silver pretty quickly at your local pawn shop but you'll be doing so at a discount.

Soft Assets: These are investments you can't really touch. Your bank account is a great example of a soft asset. Can you go down to the bank and physically touch your money? No, you can't. The bank doesn't have a little room full of dollar bills with your name on them. They keep everything in a ledger so that they know how much you've deposited and how much you've spent, but they don't have a room anywhere for you to go and count your money. That's why you can make a withdrawal from any branch—or even an ATM. Stocks and insurance are other examples of soft assets.

INVESTMENT VEHICLES

It's always a good idea to spread your investments between hard and soft assets and between liquid and illiquid assets. That way, you can virtually always access some capital if you need it for another great opportunity. Remember, this money is expected to grow and multiply, but you shouldn't siphon off any of that growth. Instead, let the growth grow, too. If you start pulling money out you'll be riding the brakes and slowing down your investment train.

Now, let's talk about types of investments and some of their pros and cons.

Real Estate: This asset class includes any kind of property fixed to the ground (typically including the ground itself, but not always). The Empire State Building is real estate held as a company (to spread the cost to a number of investors). An undeveloped plot of ground in the middle of the wilderness would also qualify as real estate. Real estate can be commercial, industrial, or residential. There are also a number of ways to make money from real estate. Some people buy and hold, waiting for the property to appreciate in value before selling again; others buy and rent, taking the monthly cash flows; still others "fix and flip," buying property, repairing any damage and making some cosmetic upgrades before selling again.

One important thing to remember about real estate is that it is largely illiquid. You can go out and buy real estate just about anywhere on just about any day of the year, but you can't turn around and sell it for the price you want at the drop of a hat. It takes time to go through the sales process even if you have an interested, able, eager buyer – and it's rare that you'll have a buyer before you list the property.

My strategy is to consider real estate as a long-term portion of your investment portfolio. Sure, you can go out and make a lot of money by "flipping" real estate (buying, holding for a short time, and selling again) in a fast market, but you are taking a big risk. As happened in 2007 and 2008, lots of people made considerable money only to be left holding the hot potato (real estate) when the music ran out and everything crashed. Most of those people went from seeming to be very rich to suddenly being very poor—often bankrupt.

Sometimes, you can go to the county office and find where the county plans to expand, then you can buy up land in that area and hold it until the growth occurs. Once other houses start going up around your land, you can usually sell it for a decent profit. But, again, it's a risk because those housing developments might not go in for years—if ever. The project can always get canceled and your kids or grandkids end up being the ones to see that growth, if they have the patience to hold the property that long.

The good news is, if your time horizon is long enough, that the world isn't getting any bigger, which means there is a finite amount of real estate. After all, "they ain't makin' anymore land." On the other hand, the world population is growing at an ever-increasing rate. Eventually, it's feasible that we'll cover every available open space on the planet—it just might take several hundred years before your land becomes valuable.

Today, there are Opportunity Zones Funds, which offer tax free gains if you hold the investment 10 years. I'm not sure how long they will last, but they are worth a good look.

Stocks and Bonds: I am no expert on this topic so I'll just say a couple of things and then let you to discuss it with your money manager. That person's job is to help you navigate the equity market. He or she is the expert, so listen to them.

Stocks are essentially partial ownership in a company. If you own one share of stock in a company that has 100 shares of stock in total, you own one percent of that company. Most companies with stock have tens of millions of shares, however, so owning a few shares only gives you fractions of a percent ownership. Still, while you may not be challenging for control of the board of directors, you can still take advantage of any growth the company may experience. If you hold one percent of the shares, your net worth grows by one percent of the company's growth.

Conversely, holding a company's stock when it falls will decrease your net worth. Again, the market is more of a long-term investment strategy. You can make some great short-term gains, but cashing out subjects you to all kinds of taxes and other penalties until you've held the stock for at least a year. Even after that, the tax laws can be confusing. Of course, just investing in stock can be confusing. There's a lot to know and that's why you need a money manager.

For instance, there are all kinds of stocks including preferred, common, voting, non-voting, dividend, non-dividend, and so forth. The various types of stocks are things to discuss with your money manager. In order to invest in stock wisely, you must really research and understand a company, its market, and its growth strategy. If you don't understand these three things you may as well go to a roulette wheel in Vegas and gamble away all your money. In addition, companies don't always make it easy to understand these three points. That's why you need a money manager. They will have a team of people doing research on the company and the market in an effort to forecast what's coming and act (buy, sell, or hold) accordingly.

The bond market allows you to act like a bank for a company or municipality. Where stocks represent ownership in a company, bonds represent IOUs from a company. The company will agree to pay out a certain interest rate and, if that sounds good to you, you can give the company cash now for the return later. As long as the company doesn't go bankrupt, you are contractually guaranteed to get all your money— plus the agreed upon interest. However, depending on how the market moves, bonds can either have an excellent return compared to other vehicles or an awful one. That's why you should diversify. Again, there are lots of different kinds of bonds, so consult your money manager for guidance.

IRAs and 401(k)s: If you are working at a company and they offer a 401(k) match, and you aren't taking it, you're a fool. If the company is willing to match 3 percent, it's basically offering you a 3 percent raise to put some money away for the future. Often, companies will match, dollar for dollar, your contributions up to a certain percentage of your annual wage. Take advantage of that. By putting in a little of your income now, you are effectively doubling that money. You will get few opportunities in life that make it so easy to double your money.

IRAs are another great investment vehicle. Depending on whether you have a Roth IRA or a traditional IRA, you can get different tax benefits. Consult a financial advisor to see what's best for you. By using these different tools, you can protect some of your income from Uncle Sam and keep more of it in your own pocket.

An IRA really serves as a shell over whatever other type of investment you put inside. Most frequently, IRAs contain savings accounts or investment accounts for stocks and bonds. However, with the right money manager and/or financial planner, it's possible to put just about anything into an IRA. You can have real estate, gold, insurance, collectibles, business ownership, etc. Again, I'm not the expert here, so go talk to a professional.

For anyone struggling to put aside that 10 percent and leave it there, IRAs and 401ks are doubly good vehicles because there are strict laws regarding when and how you can access the money. Of course, the downside to that is you can't access it to take advantage of great opportunities. Still, if you are having trouble disciplining yourself, consider using these investment vehicles to add that extra layer of protection.

Collectibles: Collectibles range from coins to stamps to art to antiques. These are typically hard assets and, for the most part, illiquid. However, collectibles can often have great upside potential. For example, I had the chance to buy, for $2,500, the painting we used on our controversial Jackson Hole phonebook cover. That painting later sold for $160,000! That one piece of art could have made me a lot of money but I passed up the opportunity. I love art, however, and have collected a lot of it over the years. Each piece I buy increases my net worth.

Collections of stamps or coins or even toys can be worthwhile as well. These kinds of items not only have and retain value, they can provide a lot of enjoyment as you hunt for the missing pieces of your collection. Antiques are often beautiful and functional. With the proper care, these kinds of things can serve as furniture for your home while still holding value and increasing your net worth. The cheap, particleboard TV stand you bought at the Megamart won't be worth anything five years from now. A beautiful, antique table from the late 1800s can actually be worth more in five years than it is now.

TV shows like "Antiques Roadshow" on PBS are all about antiques and collectibles. The whole premise of the show is that people will bring the "junk" that grandma or grandpa left behind and get it appraised. Imagine the surprise when these heirs find out that grandma's jewelry box is actually worth thousands of dollars now. Collectibles can increase your net worth more than you would expect and the better condition you keep them in, the greater their eventual worth.

Gold and Silver: In the past few years, everyone has heard about gold. There are commercials on TV all the time about investing in gold. The idea is that precious metals have been used as currency for thousands of years. Some people buy gold and hold it in case the world ends and they need currency. Others buy gold and hold it as a hedge against inflation. That's because gold will maintain its value relative to other goods and services where the dollar will not. So, if you buy some gold and set it aside, when the dollar loses value, that gold will pick up the value lost by the dollar. To demonstrate how this works, let me give you a very simple example.

Let's say you have an extra dollar and decide to buy one dollar of gold. Your friend thinks you're crazy and says it's better to hold on to the dollar so he can use it. At this point, a loaf of bread costs one dollar. Fast-forward two years through a period of intense inflation. A loaf of bread now costs two dollars. Your friend can't afford a loaf of bread anymore because he saved his dollar as a dollar. You, on the other hand, can sell your dollar in gold for two dollars—and then go buy some bread.

When the economy is in good shape and growing well, gold tends to just sit and do nothing. Gold (and other precious metals) tend to perform better when the market takes a downturn. For that reason, many people hold some precious metals in their portfolio to insulate them from down cycles. It's not a perfect protection, but it's better than nothing.

Insurance: This is an interesting topic, and one you should bring up with your money manager. Specifically here, we're talking about life insurance. Homeowner's insurance, car insurance, and health insurance are simply vehicles to protect against risk should an accident or catastrophe occur and are all mandated by law. But life insurance is different. Of course life insurance protects your family in the event that you die. My rule of thumb is that, at a bare minimum, you should have enough insurance to cover any and all debts you will leave behind —including your mortgage. Since life is an "Act of God" by the "Will of God," and He can decide to call you home at any time, it isn't fair to your loved ones to leave them with a bunch of debt or other obligations. They already have to deal with losing you. There's no reason for them to also deal with financial troubles as well. But life insurance can also be an important investment vehicle, especially if you are young enough to purchase a whole life policy because it has the potential to earn money over time.

In addition, if you already have millions in net worth, then life insurance has other benefits beyond protecting your loved ones from debt (since as a millionaire you are not likely to be in debt when you die) and as an investment vehicle. It also has estate planning and tax structuring benefits. I don't have the expertise to explain it all here (and you wouldn't want to read a book about it anyway), so talk to your financial adviser about all the ways life insurance can be a smart way to grow and protect your money.

By diversifying across different types of assets, you can help protect your wealth against fluctuations of the market and against fluctuations in your own life. You'll need trusted partners, however, and that's why you have to have a good financial adviser. If you go jumping around from one investment to another, instead of sticking with something and seeing it through, you'll quickly find that you have nothing to show for it. As the adage asserts, "A fool and his money are soon parted." Moving too quickly because you're trying to grab too many opportunities will make you a fool.

TACTICS TO INCREASE NET WORTH

There are other vehicles out there besides those I've shared. Some people like the commodities markets; some like investing in new business ventures. Perhaps you would rather invest in classic cars (though these are technically collectibles). The point is to not put all your investment money in any one category. If you do, and that category suffers a drop like the housing market did in 2008, you'll be broke. All that money you saved up will be gone, cut to a fraction of its former worth. All bubbles eventually pop. If you spread things around, however, you can minimize your losses—or even post gains during troubled times.

As far as acquiring assets, you have your money manager to help you with the soft assets, but your money manager probably doesn't specialize in hard assets like collectibles or precious metals. Additionally, you can actually purchase everyday items—like furniture—at hefty discounts and then turn around and resell them for a profit, if you know how. So let's talk about two simple tactics I've used to increase my net worth without overly increasing my network.

Bartering: Bartering was the basis for nearly all commercial exchange until a couple of hundred years ago. Money existed, but it was often in short supply and had to be minted from precious metals in order for it to have any value. Fiat money (paper currency like we have today) just wouldn't have worked because ancient societies didn't have the same commercial infrastructure that we do today. As a result, people "bought" and "sold" goods for goods, eliminating the "money" in between.

There are a number of advantages—and some disadvantages—to this basis of exchange. The first advantage is that if you do something well, you will get rewarded for that by everyone who doesn't do that same task as well. If you can grow huge pumpkins, you're going to be "rich" every Halloween. This also means that you get full benefit of any economies of scale. If you can do something more cheaply than anyone else, you get full advantage of that difference in production costs.

148

However, the danger is that your particular specialty is seasonal or obscure. If you specialize in huge pumpkins, you don't have anything to "sell" except around the fall season, meaning you can't buy anything until the fall. The whole point of cash is to make it possible to sell now and buy later (though retailers would have you believe it's so you can buy now and sell later).

Cash overcomes seasonality, but it also forces a valuation onto things that wouldn't have such an easily defined value otherwise. But if you know what you're looking for—or recognize something of value being offered for less than it's worth—you can quickly increase your net worth through bartering something that holds no value to you for something that holds much greater value. The guiding star here is that every man's trash is another man's treasure. It's getting harder to barter effectively in this age of middle management and sprawling corporations, but it's still possible. You might, for example, be able to barter consultation services to your mechanic in exchange for that new water pump your car needs. If you can make the case and show your mechanic the value, you can still do business by barter today.

Yard Sales: Yard sales are a brilliant way to increase your net worth without much work. How hard is it to wander around someone's front yard for 15 to 20 minutes? I can't tell you how many times I've found expensive or valuable items for pennies on the dollar because I was willing to stop and look around. Thrift stores operate under this same premise; they are like permanent garage sales. The best yard sales, however, are the major estate sales operated by the kids of a parent who has recently passed away.

When someone dies, they usually leave a whole lot of stuff behind. If the kids are a bit older when their parents pass, they are often more interested in the inheritance money than they are in any of the physical possessions. There are likely some heirlooms that will change hands, but often a lot of furniture or other valuables will be converted to cash and distributed evenly among the children. What's the easiest way to turn physical goods into cash? Sell at a discount. Many times, the children don't even realize the value of what they're selling—and often don't care. Their loss is your gain. If you can spend a few hours at some quality estate sales, you can increase your net worth by hundreds, or even thousands of dollars.

My best advice about increasing net worth is to learn not to constrain yourself to think that the only way to maximize your wealth is to work hard at your job and set aside more of your paycheck. Those are both good things to do but they are creating an active income that requires you to be present in order to make more money. You want to get to the point that *your money is working for you*, making you a "passive" income that doesn't require your labor in order to earn it.

Just remember that wealth comes slowly. It takes time. Those few who do manage to "get rich quick" usually get poor again just as quickly. When you work for something, you learn to value it. When you value it, you'll take care of it. So don't hurry along your path to wealth. Be patient and diligent and you'll get there.

GOALS FOR A SUCCESSFUL LIFE

THERE IS MORE TO LIFE than just making money and amassing wealth. I hope you realize that. If you haven't realized it yet, allow me to do you a favor and make that clear now: money is not happiness. Money will not bring you happiness in and of itself. Money, in fact, is typically a root cause for unhappiness. Happiness, as it turns out, is based on whether or not you can look in a mirror, stare that "other" person in the eyes, and smile.

Can you look in the mirror and be happy with what you see? Are you proud of that person's accomplishments? Are you proud of who that person is and who he or she is trying to become? If not, no amount of money is going to change things. You could inherit all of Bill Gates' fortune—tax-free—and not be any happier than you are now.

While money might make it easier to deal with the problems of life, it does not solve all of them, and is not a prescription for happiness. In fact, if you don't like the path you're on, having more money is only like pushing harder on the gas pedal. That's all money really is: an accelerant. Money will help you get where you're going more quickly. That's all. So the question isn't whether or not you have (or will have) enough money to get there. The question is whether or not you like where you're going.

So we're going to change gears a little bit now. I've taught you how to accrue wealth. You know the formula to become a millionaire. Now you need to look at the rest of your life and make sure it's on track, too; otherwise you'll just end up as a wealthy, miserable failure.

When I was in the Jaycees, as I've mentioned before, I learned a process of goal-setting that changed my life. There I was, in my early 30s, and I realized that I didn't really know what I wanted out of life. I knew, in vague terms, some of the things I wanted but I had never really sat down to figure any of that out and put it down in easily readable terms.

Everything was just ideas in my head, and—no offense—that's not a very safe place for any of us! Getting it out of your head and in writing helps you organize the path you will take.

As it turns out, we all go through phases in life—almost like seasons—wherein we slowly change from "who we were," "to who we are," "to who we will be." Often, those changes are so gradual that we don't recognize them within ourselves. We just think we're the same person we've always been when, in reality, we're completely different in almost every important way. Ideally, those changes should be improvements, but that isn't always the case. Some people slip as they get older—one wrong choice turns into another until they are buried under a snowball that turned into an avalanche. If only they could have seen the problem at the start when it was easy to fix.

Other people often notice these changes in us more than we do. They have an image of us in their heads and that image doesn't evolve as easily as we do. So friends and relatives will start to notice your changes sooner than you will. Try to listen to them if they reach out to give you advice. When they call you on something, don't get defensive; stop and consider the possibility instead.

In some ways, you have to keep a constant check on yourself, recalibrating on a regular basis. It's like maintaining a car. Some people buy a car and drive it until it falls apart, unable to understand why they always pick such awful lemons. Other people buy the same model car but they change the oil regularly, rotate the tires, perform other preventative maintenance services, and keep the tank full of gas. Why so much difference between the experience of the first car owner and the second one? Because the second person took the time to focus on the car as a machine, not just a tool. The second car owner made sure the machine stayed in good condition rather than simply trying to use it up.

Going through the goal checklist I'm about to give you—the one I received from the Jaycees—is like changing the oil and rotating the tires of your life. The list won't prevent all your problems—there's no preventative maintenance for a blown gasket—but these areas of focus will help to prevent a host of problems and keep things running smoothly. Failure to focus on these different areas in life is like passing the "Rest stop…last services for 240 miles" sign without even pausing to check your fuel gauge.

FIVE FACTORS OF FREEDOM

If you want to have balance in your life—if you want to enjoy a life in which you are wealthy—then you need to set goals in five different areas of your life: 1) mental, 2) physical, 3) spiritual, 4) social, and 5) financial. By focusing on these five areas and keeping them all in line, you can set yourself up to enjoy life—before, during, and after wealth.

I've shared this list with you a number of times already. All along, I've been trying to hint that you should be considering these areas in your own life. Now that you've come this far, I'm no longer hinting, I'm telling.

To live a truly free and balanced life, you must map out exactly where you want to be—who you want to be—in each of these areas. Then you must plot goals to take you from where you are now to where you want to go. It is vital that you not become too fixated on one area of your life at the expense of another. For example, don't set all of your goals around the financial aspect of your life. Don't set them all around the social or mental aspects either. You need to be a whole person, not just four-fifths of a person so be sure to set goals in all five areas.

Following is a review of each of these life factors:

Mental: From the day you were born, you have been learning. The human brain is about the most amazing machine anywhere. The fact that an infant can grow up and learn to talk—without any structured lessons—and then continue to develop into a full-grown adult over the space of some 20 years is mind-blowing.

Children possess a natural curiosity and desire to learn. Their ability to assimilate new information is staggering. They learn so much so quickly. And then, at age five, they start school and begin feeding those brains. Sadly, by the time kids come out of grade school, they start to feel resentful of the whole learning process. There is too much emphasis on getting the "right" answer and not enough focus on finding your own methods for getting the right answer. School, however, is the best thing we can do for kids just because of the huge amount of knowledge they can gain in such a short period of time.

After graduation, a young adult goes on to find work, or attend a trade school or university. Eventually, everyone ends up in the workforce and that's where the real problems occur. By age 35, most people are already dead—they just don't know it. They finally catch on around age 65 when they are supposed to retire and don't know what they've done with their lives. Some never catch on and just end up buried when their heart stops beating. They are working that dead-end, 9-to-5 job somewhere, and they've lost all the curiosity or interest they had as a child. The old saying is still true, "If you don't use it you lose it." You have to constantly push yourself to learn new things or your brain will shut down.

Make sure to set goals that will force you to continue learning and expanding your mind. In the end, you brain is the best asset you have. Everything else you do will come because of what you did to utilize your brain.

Physical: It's interesting to me that as kids we were given nap time and recess at school. We were basically forced to get more sleep and have more physical activity. Now that we're grown up, most people's work allows for neither. We're pushed faster and faster every day. There's no time to sleep, much less exercise, and eating homemade, healthy food is a burden as often as not. Is it any wonder that according to the Centers for Disease Control, 35.7 percent of the American adult population is obese? That number, by the way, doesn't include all the adults that are overweight, just obese.

Sleep is another issue. As we get older, we need less sleep than when we were younger, but everybody still needs sleep. You should allow yourself eight hours of sleep each night. If you cut that short, you are cutting hours off your life. Sleep deprivation causes poor performance at work, which can cost you that promotion and also brings a number of other physical and mental problems with it. Some companies nowadays are starting to implement workplace napping policies in an effort to help employees stay more productive and engaged with their awake time.

Without physical balance, you can't really have balance in the other areas of life. So what can you do to improve your physical self? What goals can you set? Can you park the car a little farther from the front door of the store when you run your errands? Can you take the stairs instead of the elevator? Can you do more walking or jogging when you need to go around the neighborhood, rather than taking the car two blocks over? It's amazing how much exercise a person can get in a day without specifically going to "work out."

Social: None of us came to earth to live alone in a cave. Humans are social creatures by nature. We have been in packs, tribes, villages, and neighborhoods since the dawn of time. Even in the remote jungles of the world where native populations still live the same way people lived thousands of years ago, they live in societies.

As a human, you have an innate need to satisfy your social side. Some people are more social that others, I'll admit, but everyone needs a friend or two, and everyone needs some time to communicate with others once in a while. You can't live like a hermit and have a fulfilled, happy life. If you isolate yourself and live only in tiny compartments—church, family, work—you will end up unfulfilled. You need to be open to associating with others, especially those you don't know. You have lots to offer them and you need to be willing to offer it.

Once again, John Donne got it right: "No man is an island." If we try to be an island, we will end up lonely and miserable. Even nations need to understand this principle in today's world. If they did, we wouldn't have so many problems and so much strife.

Spiritual: Life is far too amazing to take for granted. Shakespeare's character Hamlet, who was a student at Wittenberg, said to his friend: "There are more things in heaven and earth, Horatio, than are dreamt of in your philosophy" (Act 1, Scene 5). This comment comes after they see the ghost of Hamlet's father. In short, we can't explain everything scientifically. Like it or not, we all have a spiritual dimension. My challenge to you is to find it and embrace it.

Whether you believe in God or not, you have a need to periodically charge your spirit. For most people this involves some kind of communion with a higher power. At the least, it should involve some quiet contemplation and meditation. The spiritual aspect of your life is really a factor of your ability to live with yourself. Are you at peace with what you've done and the way you've done it? At the end of the day, you need to be able to look yourself in the mirror and meet your own eyes. That's spirituality. In the same way that you need mental balance and physical fitness, you need spiritual balance or you will never find peace and happiness.

Financial: This is the aspect of life we've been working on for the past five lessons. While this particular aspect of life is probably the least important to your overall happiness (so long as your needs are met), it provides the catalyst whereby you can meet all your other goals. Without sufficient financial resources, it can be harder to achieve the important goals in the other areas of your life. And while wealth for wealth's sake is unimportant, wealth is important for the freedom it grants you to act. If you want to make more of yourself and be a blessing to others, you need the resources to make it happen. This doesn't mean that you can't live a balanced life unless you're wealthy, but it is certainly easier to balance your life once your finances are no longer a pressing concern.

MAINTAIN BALANCE OR BUST

In order to have real balance in your life, you need to be pursuing goals in all five of these areas. With that in mind, let me give you a little advice regarding goals: an aspiration isn't a goal until you write it down. Until you are willing to write down your goals you'll likely not go into enough detail to really understand what you're asking of yourself. How often have you had an idea that made perfect sense in your head, only to try to explain it to someone else and fall short? Our brains are excellent at jumping to conclusions and making connections between seemingly random ideas. Once we try to explain those connections, however, we sometimes have trouble, revealing the weaknesses or insufficiencies in our ideas. By writing down your goals, you take the first step toward clearing up the weak spots.

I recommend that you write down at least ten goals for each one of the five categories and then refer to that list frequently to remind yourself of your goals. They don't need to all be big, world-changing goals. Some should be small and take only a small stretch to reach. Some can even be recurring, like an exercise or fitness goal. Others should be very long-term in nature so that you have something to push for throughout your life. Any time you achieve one of your goals, cross it off the list and create a new one to replace it. Make realistic goals whenever possible, not just a wish list, and plan out the steps for how you will accomplish them.

Also, I encourage you to not only plan your goals, but plan your rewards as well. Crossing off an achievement will be a reward in itself, but also find a prudent and balanced way to reward yourself. Don't go "hog-wild" and destroy everything you've worked so hard to build. Celebrate your successes—appropriately!

I cannot stress enough that, to be truly successful, you must balance yourself regularly in each of the five areas. You cannot let yourself get out of balance even though you will be naturally inclined to slip out of balance as you go through life. That means it takes effort and attention to stay in balance.

If you ever get lost, stop right where you are and evaluate the situation. It's better to lose a little time sorting things out than to push forward and find out later that you were on the wrong path all along. Get back to the basics on a regular basis. This might require you to back-track somewhat, but going down just any road will lead you to just any destination. If you want to get to New York, you probably shouldn't be hopping a flight to Mexico City. Figure out where you're going and then go there.

I know I've said this ten different ways, but just in case you missed it: If you can't balance yourself and keep your life on track, all the wealth in the world will only serve to destroy you. Keep balanced. Focus yourself equally mentally, physically, socially, spiritually, and financially.

KEEP BALANCED OR ELSE

L ESSON 6 WAS THE MOST IMPORTANT lesson I've taught you so far. Lessons 1 through 5 were really all about learning to amass wealth. I've had plenty of people take those lessons to heart and do very well for themselves. Unfortunately, some of those people only got rich; they never developed true wealth. True wealth is more than just money in the bank. True wealth is more than just being a money hoarder – becoming Mr. Scrooge isn't the point of these lessons.

I call these lessons the "Life Lessons," not the "Lessons of Wealth" for a reason. The reason is that money alone doesn't bring happiness. I've said that to you a number of times now, but it can't be stressed enough. If you want happiness, you need to seek balance in life, as I emphasized in Lesson 6. The times when I've been out of balance have been the times of the greatest hardship for me—like starting out in college, working as a conservation officer, and going through my divorce. It's no coincidence that on average, my life got a lot better after I got involved with the Jaycees and started living their creed.

You can't have happiness without balance. That's why you need to have a constant, careful eye on your course. I've learned to fly airplanes in my life and one of the things I've learned is that it's easy to get off course—even by just a little, especially when flying over mountains. The wind can come from different directions and take you by complete surprise. If you're not careful, you can get knocked way off course without even realizing it. It's natural to be pushed off course, so don't think that you're some kind of failure if it happens; just get back on course as quickly as you can.

When you find yourself off course, take a deep breath, look at the situation, refer back to your goals, and get back in the saddle. Sometimes it will be easier than other times, especially if you've let yourself get far off course because it's been a while since you checked your map. The more often you check on your path, the easier it will be to stay on course.

That's the purpose of setting goals in each of the five categories. Those goals will provide that map for you to follow when life starts to feel unmanageable. And be sure to review your goals periodically. It's no good to be pushing for a goal you wrote down 10 years ago if you don't still feel the same way now. Sometimes, as you age, goals will move forever out of reach. Other goals will move within reach, however, so it all evens out. In this review process, be sure to look at all your goals. You can't afford to get too caught up in one or two goals at a time. If you do, life will blindside you from one of the other areas and knock you way off balance.

Focusing on just a single goal would be like driving a car with a focus on just one gauge on your dashboard. You can watch your speedometer all day, but it you don't pay attention to the fuel gauge, you're going to end up running out of gas. If you watch just the fuel gauge and not the tachometer, you'll end up burning up your engine when you should be shifting gears. And no one should ignore the temperature gauge. Once that needle starts to move, it moves fast, and can move with tragic results. If you aren't careful, you'll cook your engine and get set way back.

PERSONAL FITNESS

With that need for balance in mind, let me highlight the need for physical fitness. In the time I have been giving these lessons, this seems to be the area where people have the easiest time "forgetting" their goals. Maybe it's because, like a car, we don't want to pay attention until there's a problem. The danger with that mode of thinking is that just like a car, preventative maintenance is fairly cheap but fixing a real problem tends to be quite expensive.

We each received a body when we were born, and everyone's body is a bit different. Some are large, others are small. Some are short or tall or pale or dark or whatever. What most people don't focus on is that, unlike a car, you only get one body. Period. You can't trade up for the new model year just because you don't like how smoothly (or not) your body is running. When a body starts to break down, it takes that person a lot of work and sometimes a lot of money to turn things around (if they can be turned around at all). For that reason, you need to take care of your body. You have to live in it (hopefully for a long time), so you need it to be clean and well-functioning.

Additionally, few things in life can get you down or off track as quickly as issues with your health. When your body is functioning properly, you almost don't even notice it. When something goes wrong, it will send your whole life into a spin. If you keep your body fit, you will largely avoid a whole host of problems. If you choose not to keep your body in shape, you are choosing to play roulette with your health—and your life.

The older you get, the more difficult it is to keep your body in shape and healthy. Decisions you make now will impact you for years into the future. If you choose to be healthy now—and do what it takes to make that a reality—you will reap the benefits of that health into the future. If you choose not to be healthy now, you will suffer those consequences in the future. Keep this in mind with regard to substance abuse too. Drugs, alcohol, tobacco, coffee and other things may seem like the only way to get through your challenges right now, but you'll pay the price later. You wouldn't dump trash in the gasoline you put in your car; why would you dump trash in your body?

YOUR ROADMAP

You need that roadmap—your list of goals—to keep you on track so you can avoid the pitfalls of life. Remember the quote from Alexander Hamilton: "If you don't stand for something, you'll fall for anything." Your goals serve to remind you what you stand for. If you don't write them down and reread them often, you will fall for anything. You'll end up jumping from path to path in search of happiness because you aren't actually sure what you want in life.

Deep down, you'll be driven to find happiness, but you won't have a map to find the way. The only thing you can directly change in life is you. By changing yourself, you may change your environment, and you will certainly influence those around you, but you can only change you directly.

Everything else is changed indirectly through your influence. In a world where many marriages end in failure, children are experimenting at younger and younger ages, higher education is getting more expensive and more mandatory, and corporate loyalty to the employee (and vice versa) is at an all-time low, it's nice to know that you still have control of yourself and that you're on track to become who you want to be.

There is no greater peace in life than being at peace with yourself and with your Maker. If you can manage those two things, you can handle whatever life throws at you. It doesn't matter what other people think about you. Their opinions are just that: theirs. Their opinions only influence your opinion if you let them. Be confident in who and what you are and ignore what other people think. You know your course, and you're going to follow that course; let other people worry about their own paths.

If you stick to your goals, life will smooth out in time. The bumps will never fully go away, but you'll be able to handle the bumps because you're confident in yourself. So be happy with yourself and work to make your situation a happy place. If you can do those two things, the world can never throw a big enough problem at you to get you off track for long. You'll be too sure in your foundation.

And don't worry about making mistakes. It's going to happen. In fact, when you're doing your best, you're more likely to make mistakes because you are committing yourself to a course of action and pushing forward. People who tread water don't make mistakes, but they don't progress either. So learn to look at your inevitable mistakes as stepping stones. Each mistake will carry you a little higher, teach you a little more, and help you end up wiser than you were before. Just remember to move forward. Don't let a simple mistake keep you down. Stick to your goals, push forward, and you'll make progress and have success like you never thought possible.

TAKING CONTROL
OF YOUR OWN FATE

FIRST OF ALL, CONGRATULATIONS are in order. If you've followed my suggestions and are applying the lessons I have recommended, you are in the 10 percent of people who ever make changes to their financial life. Most really want to start the process because they really want to become millionaires, and they start the first lesson or two with a lot of enthusiasm. As the lessons require more commitment and effort, however, most people eventually stop coming back to me to ask for the next lesson. Most of them probably go look for an "easier" way to earn success. I wish them luck, but I don't hold out much hope. There is no such thing as getting rich quick—and it usually ends in tragedy if it happens at all.

I recognize that these lessons require changes to old habits, and that's not easy for most people, but I know that anyone can follow this process if they really want to. The biggest drop off occurs after Lesson 4 when I instruct people to find a financial advisor. Interestingly, this step is really as simple as finding a doctor you can trust when you have a life-threatening illness. If you knew you were dying, wouldn't you work to find a doctor who could help you right away? Money managers are like doctors. You can also look at them like personal trainers who will help you get financially fit.

In keeping with that analogy, remember that you aren't going to like every doctor on the planet—or every personal trainer—and that not all are created equally. You need to find a person you can trust, someone who does business in a way you understand. One of the easiest ways to find this out is to meet the money manager and interview him or her just like you'd interview a job candidate. As part of that process, be sure to ask for references and follow through to check on those references.

If you'll follow the steps I've given you up to this point, you'll be well on your way to becoming a millionaire—if you haven't crossed that bar already. More importantly, if you continue to learn from these lessons, you'll continue to be a millionaire. Congratulations on that, too. The next question is what to do next.

You have two real options at this point: A) you can stay the course, continue to follow the previous lessons, and continue to grow your wealth slowly; or B) you can accelerate things to the next level. If you choose Option A I wish you all the best. You've done a great job and you and your money manager can make wonderful things happen. Go ahead and skip the rest of this lesson. To those who are willing to pick Option B and do whatever it takes to accelerate your wealth generation, keep reading.

WEALTH ACCELERATION

So far, I've given you the necessary lessons to help you become a millionaire—a happy millionaire who can hold on to that wealth instead of blowing it. I've done what I can to help you into the top 10 percent of Americans, in terms of wealth. If you want to reach the one percent club in America, you must be willing to leverage everything you have. You must be willing to risk it all in an effort to make your wealth grow exponentially. Think you're ready for that kind of commitment? Here's the next step for you: start or buy a business.

You'll never make it into the top one percent unless you are running a business. A few Fortune 500 CEOs have made enough to get into this group, but many have not. Usually, those who make it into the top one percent are those who start or buy a small business, grow it, and then sell it for 10, 100, or even 1,000 times what they spent on getting it started.

If you think back to the nature of wealth, most of it is not held as cash in the bank; it's held as ownership interest in businesses. The real money and wealth in the economy is held in the business sphere, not in personal savings accounts at the local bank. If you want to tap into that market and claim that wealth, you need a business vehicle to get there.

Unfortunately, the risks are high. Approximately half of all business ventures fail without really getting off the ground. And the risks don't end there. Many people will create a viable business, grow it, have some really good times, and then hold on too long and try to go too far. These people ride the business all the way up and then back down again. Part of the reason for that is because for a person to be willing to take the risk on starting a business in the first place, that person must have a high tolerance for risk. Then, once you've been through the storms a business can throw at you, it's hard to step back and let go.

I would guess that only about one percent of people are willing to take the risk and bet it all to start a business. Is it any wonder, then, that only one percent of people control so much more wealth than everyone else? Interestingly, once a person can build a successful business, usually only health or death can pull that person out of the game. So few successful entrepreneurs sell that first business and then really retire. Most of them leverage all that new wealth into new ventures in an effort to continue growing. I've known people who were so good at growing wealth that they were on death's doorstep and still calling the shots because they just couldn't let go.

That's the reason I gave you Lesson 6. If you take my advice and go on this journey, you'll either win big or lose big. Either way, keeping those goals in mind will help keep your priorities straight. If you let yourself get caught up in the business to the exclusion of your other goals, you'll look back and be dissatisfied.

WHAT, WHEN, AND WHERE

If you've decided to take the challenge and run your own business, there are a couple of additional considerations. First, what kind of business do you want to run? This question is a personal one, and I really can't answer it for you. I have knowledge about certain types and styles of businesses, so I look to invest in those kinds of companies. You will be drawn to business in the same way—to your own specialty. Do whatever it is you dream of doing. Don't try to pick a business just because someone else told you it's a good deal. Remember, no matter what kind of business you end up running, your goal is to build it up and then sell it. If you try to build it up to hand it down to a family member or for any other reason, you're making a mistake.

Also be cautious about economic "bubbles." As an economy grows, people will try to predict the future and invest where they think the growth will happen. If you've been following my lessons to this point, you are one of those people. Sometimes, that growth can seem so exciting that it draws a disproportionate amount of attention and investment. Eventually, people will start to pull back because they recognize that the fundamentals no longer support the excitement. At that point, the bubble will burst.

Make sure that your business is ready for things like that. Again, pick a business that does something you either know or love. Don't pick an industry just because it seems like it's on the upward swing. Too many fortunes have been lost on betting that the bubble will keep growing only to find that it popped the next day.

As to the question of when to start your business, that time is now. Not tomorrow, not yesterday, right now. That said, you don't have to go out and get a business license today. Before starting Phone Directories Company, I spent hours listening to motivational tapes (yes tapes, not CDs), reading books about starting businesses, and talking to others in a number of different industries. I recognized the importance of education even though my formal education had little relation to running a business. In fact, when I finally started my business, I was at a disadvantage because I had no real experience about how businesses worked. I made a lot of mistakes at the beginning that cost me a lot of time and money and put a lot of stress on my family. Still, I was able to pull through and survive, so I know you can, too.

When you finally start your business, be prepared to go at least three years without bringing a paycheck home because you will be turning every last penny back into the business. If you start taking your own paycheck too soon, you'll end up siphoning off money that you needed for growth and expansion. At first, it will seem like everything is draining you of cash —you may think that just one more purchase will get you a leg up on the competition and take you to a place where you can be stable and start cranking out success. Don't be fooled.

I can only compare starting a business to my years as a conservation officer. When you start to climb a mountain you naturally look up and can see the top. It probably doesn't even look that far away. Then, as you start to hike up to that peak, the trail is quite pleasant and you've got lots of energy. But before long you begin to get a bit tired and start to gauge how much farther until you reach the top—except that you probably can't see the peak anymore. Instead, what looks like the peak turns out to be just a ridge on the way up. You climb over that and get a glimpse of the real peak before you start climbing for the next ridge and the next view. Then, after all that effort, you finally reach the peak and realize that it's just the first in a string of progressively taller peaks. So you start down a little, hike across the saddle, and start climbing again. In growing a business, there is no relenting and no relief until you suddenly find yourself at the top. It's a magical, brief moment, and then you're working toward the next milestone again. The whole process can seem overwhelming and exhausting.

Thankfully, there is no better place to start a business than here in America – especially a small business. This country is built on small businesses that employ, on average, about 10 people. So decide where your passion lies, begin studying, and get your business going. If you really want to generate wealth, building your own business and then selling it is the only way to do it.

THE HOME STRETCH:
DRIVING TO THE FINISH LINE

B Y NOW, YOUR WHOLE VIEW of income and net-worth should be fundamentally changed. You should be rock solid in your commitment to save more than 10 percent of each paycheck. You should be well on your way to getting your business started or purchasing one. You should have goals set and a financial adviser to help you reach them.

I hope that you've found the first eight lessons to be helpful. I'm sure you've made some unexpected and fortunate advances and avoided some unexpected pitfalls. I consider these lessons to be the foundation upon which a quality life can be built. I learned these lessons for myself by living life. Some of the ideas came from mentors, but most just came from living and learning. The school of hard knocks is a hard teacher, but I was a hard student, so it all worked out. I just hope that some of you will learn my lessons and avoid some of the mistakes I made.

I sometimes catch myself wondering where I would be in life if I hadn't made so many mistakes. Not that I want to go back and change my life; I've met my goals and lived a good life, but part of me wonders how much further along I could be. But then I remind myself that mistakes are the greatest teachers. We all make mistakes—some bigger than others—so don't dwell on that so much. Making mistakes doesn't make you a mistake. You can be a good person even if you sometimes make the wrong choice. The key is to learn from those mistakes, pick yourself back up, and keep going. Then, in time and in turn, you need to pass along that wisdom and knowledge to help others avoid your mistakes and take advantage of your successes.

At some point, you—like everyone else—will reach a ripe old age and pass on. What will be your legacy? Have you thought about your exit strategy as you enter the home stretch? Are you going to just leave all the planning to your children? Or are you going to set your house in order before you go? Hopefully, you've used (or will use) your net worth to improve the lives of those around you, not just your own. In either case, what do you want that net worth to do once you're gone? Death can spell disaster in a wealthy family if things aren't set up properly or if proper expectations aren't set.

WHERE WILL THE NET WORTH GO?

If you learned the lessons soon enough in life, you should have had ample time to build a healthy retirement. I certainly hope that's the case. Whether you've reached retirement or not, however, there's one more thing you need to do for that net worth you're taking care of: you need to decide what happens to that value when you pass on.

I know this may feel like either a morbid topic or, if you're young enough, an irrelevant topic. Regardless of how you feel about estate planning, however, the fact is that you never know when your time is coming. It could be tomorrow, or it could be in 50 years. None of us knows the answer to that question. And, even if you don't pass on for a number of years, life expectancies nowadays are longer than mental health expectancies. The best thing you can do is plan now, while you're still in complete control of yourself.

With that in mind, let me make five suggestions for what you can do to prepare your net worth for the day when it passes on to others.

1. Start now. Life doesn't last forever, and all bubbles burst.

Now, while you're in the good years of your life, set things in order for the end and what happens after. It's not like you can't adjust those plans once they're set. In fact, adjusting those plans at the last minute is much easier that trying to build them from scratch. We've all played the game of musical chairs. Life is great while the music is playing, but you don't want to be the one without a seat when the music stops. Have your plan ready and you won't have to worry about where the chairs are when the music stops—yours will be all staked out and ready for you (and your posterity).

2. Have a trusted attorney help you draft a will.

In basic terms, a will sets out your intentions for your possessions after you pass. Who will get what? How much? When? A will is used by the court system to determine how to distribute your assets after you pass. In effect, you give the court system a blueprint to follow in an effort to make sure that things end up the way you want them to. It's not foolproof, but it's a critical first step. Also keep in mind that a will can be changed and updated throughout your life, so it's never too early to write one.

The reason you want to involve a trusted lawyer is because wills can be contested in court and, in today's sue-happy society, often are. Having a well-crafted will can help to ensure that your legacy is left the way you want it. If you write your own will without the help of a legal professional, you increase the chance that something in it will be struck down by the courts, thereby striking down that portion of your legacy.

In addition, if you have minor children, you want to be sure to have a will in place that states who will be the legal guardian of those children in case both you and your spouse pass away. If you do not have a will in place, the state will take custody of your minor children, regardless of any relatives that may come forward willing to take care of them, and their ultimate fate will be decided by the courts and not by you.

3. Set up a trust in order to avoid probate.
The state ruins every funeral it attends.

Once you have a will, the next step is to create a trust. In the eyes of the government, a trust is an entity unto itself—almost like its own person. The difference is that trusts can't really die since they aren't really people. In that manner, they are almost more like businesses. The idea behind a trust is that it can have changeable leadership and you can control who those leaders are and under what circumstances they change.

Let's say you've spent your whole life building up your net worth and establishing a plan for your legacy. You've even made your will. Then you pass on. Your estate (everything you've left behind) will go to probate court. Depending on the laws of your state, anyone can go in and request to be the executor of your estate. Anyone. The courts aren't likely to accept people unless they can prove some sort of connection to you, but anyone can apply. The executor is responsible for acting out the final wishes contained in your will—within reason.

So what happens when someone (maybe a child or grandchild, maybe an old business partner) steps up and wins the right to be your executor and then that person violates your will and does something else with your estate? Your family can step in and take that person to court, but the results are never pleasant.

You can avoid that kind of situation by appointing your own successor trustee—through the use of a trust. If you only have a will in place, the court will pick your executor if your estate goes to probate. You can list your selection in your will, and the court will consider your wishes, but the decision still goes to the court. If you have a trust, however, the decision remains yours. This isn't to say that trusts are above legal challenge, but a properly established trust formed during your lifetime has a lot more legal strength.

Your trust will include your will but can do so in a much more specific way. You can list not only the distribution of assets but also the methods of distribution and who should manage that process. And since a trust can be set up as a living document, you can still retain the right to change, add, or subtract things as you go through life. Basically, you give control of all your net worth to your trust and then you keep control of the trust—thereby keeping control of all your net worth.

4. Remember that estate planners and money managers aren't the same people–though they probably know one another.

Your money manager has been helping you grow your net worth. Hopefully, that partner has been of great value to you and will hopefully continue to be of great value. Now you have reached a point to involve yet another partner in your personal executive-management team. As you plan for the latter phases of life and beyond, you need to reach out to an estate planner. In all likelihood, your estate planner will not be your money manager. In fact, they can't be the same person. An effective money manager has a different perspective and skill set than an estate planner—though the two are somewhat complementary.

The process for selecting your estate planner is much the same as the process for selecting a money manager. You need to interview several people, get references, check backgrounds, and feel out priorities. Make sure that your estate planner is a personality match for you. After all, this person will be looking over your net worth for the rest of your life, and beyond.

During this process, the concept of life insurance will undoubtedly come up. Will you invest in life insurance? If so, where will the proceeds go? Will you have the money go to your spouse? Children? Grandchildren? Some other person or cause? Nearly anything is possible, so you need to make sure to discuss these things with your estate planner. Listen to your planner's advice and then have that person help you make your own plans. You don't have to do anything and everything your estate planner recommends, but remember that the person has studied and trained to give good recommendations. If you are careful in the recruitment process, you should be able to trust the advice of your planner.

5. Remember that this is the Journey of Life, *not* the Destination of Death.

You still have a race to run! Granted, you are in the home stretch. So, plan for the future, but live for now.

Don't spend all your time worrying about what will happen when you go. Do what you can to prepare for that day and remember that an ounce of prevention is worth a pound of cure. Once you've prepared, focus on what life you have left. Spend it doing the things you have always dreamed of doing. You have your goals from Lesson 6, so live them. Don't be one of those people who gets death and retirement in the wrong order.

With the advances in medical technology today, you can live a vibrant life well after retirement age. You may not have the same stamina as you did in your youth—you probably aren't as handsome or beautiful either—but you never have to give up your motivation or willpower. As long as you are in control of yourself, take control. Don't sit around and wait to get buried. Enjoy today, and then enjoy tomorrow too. Your time will come when it comes. Don't worry about that. You've already planned for it.

I like what Jimmy Buffett says: "I'd rather die while I'm living than live when I'm dead."

INHERITANCE AND EXPECTATION

As we wrap up this lesson, I'd like to give you one last bit of advice. Over the years, I've seen countless families torn apart by the death of a parent. Sadly, it's not the grief that does it; it's the squabbling over the estate afterward. Part of the problem is that the surviving family members are already emotionally exhausted from the grief. Then, in that highly emotional state, they have to dismantle everything the deceased family member built and distribute the proceeds.

This process inevitably leads to more heartache as precious heirlooms are sold or, sometimes, stolen (usually by a family member who wasn't supposed to receive the item in the first place). Sometimes a spouse of one of the children will seize the opportunity to try to secure a larger portion of the inheritance, stirring anger and resentment among the children. In some cases, this can drive a family apart permanently. Sometimes the fallout can be so bad that the children refuse to speak to each other ever again. I know it might seem a bit extreme but I've seen it happen.

Money changes people, as I've said before. When I sold my company I made everyone on my executive team millionaires, if they weren't already. They all started out with a lot of money. Only a few were wise with that sudden lump sum of cash. Most spent it on frivolous things. A few of them spent it so quickly that they felt they should have received more; they ended up worse off than they would have been had the gotten no payout in the first place.

In a very real sense, these people received an inheritance from me. Figuratively, the company "died" and left them with a large lump sum. A few managed that money wisely; most did not. Children in a family are the same way. When given a lump-sum inheritance, a few might manage it properly, the rest will not. Of those who do not, most will have fun with it and move on with life much as they were before. A small percentage, however, will burn through it so quickly (maybe they burned through it before they even received it) that they will start to resent the parent. They will also start to resent the siblings who still have some money.

If you think back to Lesson 1 and the video I asked you to watch, 90 percent of society just doesn't understand how to handle money. It runs through their hands just as quickly as they can grab it up. That same inability to manage money applies to children as well. Most of them won't know how to hold on to inheritance money, and in many cases, having a large sum of money for even a short time can ruin them for life. We both know that's not what you want for your beneficiaries.

As a parent, your job is to learn the skills to create net worth and then teach those skills to your children. You should be teaching them to be responsible, to be frugal, to gain education, and to work hard. You need to teach your children that there is no such thing as a free lunch.

Even in my sunset years, I can still remember the advice of my father: "If you work harder than the guy next to you, you'll never go hungry." That means you need to be willing to let your children make mistakes and then find their own way out again. If you always rush in and rescue them, you are simply crippling them. One day, you won't be around. Who will rush in and rescue your child then? Teach them to rescue themselves. Teach them to work harder than the guy next to them so they never have to go hungry, even if they do get something from you in the end. They must learn to work hard and amass their own net worth. If you try to just give it to them, you're simply giving them a free lunch (or a lot of free lunches). Eventually, that free lunch will run out, and what happens if that child learned dependency on the resources you left behind? As the saying goes: "A fool and his money are soon parted."

My philosophy is to leave something personal and sentimental to each child. Leave each one a special heirloom to remember you by, and then give each one a small nest egg – just enough to get them started, take the edge off a bad start, or secure them for a rainy day or two. Don't ever give them enough to teach them dependency on the gift. The heirloom will give them a way to remember you and the lessons you taught. The small inheritance will give them a boost without removing their personal responsibility to provide for themselves.

In doing this, I give you another warning: be sure to be transparent with your children. As you amass your net worth, your children will probably recognize the wealth you now control. They may not, but they likely will. If they begin to guess at your worth and then do the math, they may begin to expect a large sum of money. Over time, that expectation will root into their souls, and they may go so far as to act like the prodigal son and spend the worth—in this case before it's even theirs. Don't give them the chance to live that world of fantasy. Instead, be clear about your plans and what you intend to leave. Set that expectation early so that they understand what they will—and will not—receive.

Consider the examples of most of the super-wealthy today. Bill Gates and Warren Buffett have each publicly explained what they want to have happen with their massive fortunes after they die. Their children will get respectable sums, but being a child of one of these two is not a free ticket to being a billionaire. And that expectation has been set by them and made abundantly clear. Do the same for your own children. Let them know what to expect; don't let them expect to get it all.

STAY THE COURSE: "RONNIE! DON'T FALL OFF!"

ONE OF MY FAVORITE MOVIES is Secretariat. I'm sure you've all seen it. If you haven't, go watch it on Netflix or Amazon or buy the CD. It is worth watching. It's all about what we have been talking about: aligning your life, prioritizing, risk taking, running your race, and understanding what real wealth is.

When Penny Chenery was about to lose the farm, Secretariat was worth $6,000,000—exactly what the declining horse estate needed to stay out of debt. Challenging the male establishment, Penny went out and syndicated the horse at $6,080,000. This was a big risk. Her brother and her husband were not happy. They were more concerned about the money, what the estate might bring to them, and avoiding risk. Penny is quoted as saying, "My father's legacy is not his money. My father's legacy is the will to win."

If you know the story, Secretariat—with Ronnie Turcotte aboard—won the final Triple Crown race by 31 lengths over his nearest competitor, Sham. Can you imagine that? Thirty-one lengths? As he hit the straightaway, Lucien Laurin the trainer, is quoted as saying, "Ronnie! Don't fall off!"

You've run a good race up to this point. You've overcome obstacles that you could not foresee. You've had highs and lows—and everything in between. What do I mean by that? I mean everything! In my faith we talk about avoiding pride and every appearance of evil. Don't get full of yourself. Don't think you are immune to the foibles, frailties and temptations of the average human. I know I am speaking "covertly." That said, you get my drift.

Let me put it one more way.

Robert Frost said, take "the road less traveled, [for] that has made all the difference." Don't take the road that everyone else takes. Keep expectations for yourself—the professional, personal and spiritual—high. I have seen people get to this point and lose all they have to divorce, infidelity and other disasters of their own making.

I know this seems odd for a lesson that is supposed to be about wealth acquisition, but, remember, these are life lessons as well.

To win, you have to stay the course and finish the race—all the way to finish line.

So, Ronnie or Sue or Jack or Jill or whoever you are out there. You're in the home stretch, so, *don't fall off!*